Uncollected Poems and Prose

Poet, translator, folklorist, A.K. Ramanujan was elected to the American Academy of Arts and Sciences in 1990; he won a Padma Shri in 1976, a Mac Arthur Fellowship in 1981, and a posthumous prize from the Sahitya Akademi for *Collected Poems*. From his first book of poems, *The Striders*, which was a Poetry Book Society Choice, Ramanujan has never lacked exceptional readers. Now a decade after his death, his reputation has steadily grown. In increasing numbers, his essays, poems, and translations, are receiving worldwide attention from students, academics, and editors of anthologies. This volume brings to you, poems and essays that could not be published in his lifetime. Included are two separate interviews. In them, Ramanujan speaks about exile, the politics of language, and about being a trilingual translator and a bilingual poet. The poems have an immediacy that is hard to resist; and the essay 'Ring of Memory, on Remembering and Forgetting in Indian Literature', opens up a new interdisciplinary field of inquiry.

A.K. RAMANUJAN (1919–1993) was William E. Colvin Professor at the University of Chicago. He translated from Classic Tamil and Medieval Kannada (*The Interior Landscape, Speaking of Siva, Poems of Love and War, Hymns for the Drowning, Folktales from India, The Flowering Tree*); and he wrote poems in English (*The Striders, Relations, Second Sight, The Black Hen*). A collection of his poems and translations, *The Oxford India Ramanujan* was published by OUP in 2004, and shortly, there will be an exciting new volume containing three books of poems and a novella, translated from Kannada into English titled, *Someone Else's Autobiography*.

MOLLY DANIELS-RAMANUJAN is the author of three works of fiction, and two books of criticism: *G.V. Desani, Writer and Worldview*, and *The Prophetic Novel*.

KEITH HARRISON, poet and translator, is Professor Emeritus at Carleton College, Northfield, Minnesota.

W0229974

Books in English by A.K. Ramanujan

Poetry

The Striders (1966)
Relations (1971)
Selected Poems (1976)
Second Sight (1986)
Collected Poems (1995)

Translations

The Interior Landscape: Love Poems from a Classical Tamil Anthology (1967)
Speaking of Śiva, Kannada bhakti poem by Vīraśaiva saints (1973)
Saṃskarā: A Rite for a Dead Man, a Kannada Novel by U. Anantha Murthy (1976)
Hymns for the Drowning: Poems for Viṣṇu by Nammāḻvār, translated from Tamil (1981)
Poems of Love and War: From the Eight Anthologies and the Ten Long Poems of Classical Tamil (1985)
Folktales from India: A Selection of Oral Tales from Twenty-two Languages (1991)

Co-authored and co-edited with others

The Literatures of India: An Introduction, with Edward C. Dimock Jr., and others (1974)
Another Harmony: New Essays on the Folklore of India (1986), with Stuart Blackburn
When God Is a Customer: Telugu Courtesan Songs by Kṣetrayya and Others (1994), with V. Narayana Rao and David Shulman
The Oxford Anthology of Modern Indian Poetry (1994), with Vinay Dharwadker

Posthumous

The Black Hen in the Collected Poems (1995)
The Flowering Tree (1996) and Other Oral Tales from India (1997)
Collected Essays (1999)
Uncollected Poems and Prose (2000)

A.K. Ramanujan

Uncollected Poems and Prose

Edited by
Molly Daniels-Ramanujan
Keith Harrison

OXFORD
UNIVERSITY PRESS

OXFORD
UNIVERSITY PRESS

Oxford University Press is a department of the University of Oxford.
It furthers the University's objective of excellence in research, scholarship,
and education by publishing worldwide. Oxford is a registered trademark of
Oxford University Press in the UK and in certain other countries

Published in India by
Oxford University Press
22 Workspace, 2nd Floor, 1/22 Asaf Ali Road, New Delhi 110002, India

© Oxford University Press 2001

'A Good Man's Dying' by Helen Singer © 1959, The Poetry Foundation
reprinted by permission of Poetry
'Invisible Bodies' by A.K. Ramanujan © 1994, The New Yorker

The moral rights of the authors have been asserted

First Edition published in 2001
Oxford India Paperbacks 2005
21st impression 2022

All rights reserved. No part of this publication may be reproduced, stored in
a retrieval system, or transmitted, in any form or by any means, without the
prior permission in writing of Oxford University Press, or as expressly permitted
by law, by licence, or under terms agreed with the appropriate reprographics
rights organization. Enquiries concerning reproduction outside the scope of the
above should be sent to the Rights Department, Oxford University Press, at the
address above

You must not circulate this work in any other form
and you must impose this same condition on any acquirer

ISBN-13: 978-0-19-567291-6
ISBN-10: 0-19-567291-7

Typeset in Sabon MT
by Eleven Arts, Delhi 110 035
Printed in India by Manipal Technologies Limited, Manipal

CONTENTS

—◆◆◆◆—

TWO INTERVIEWS

UNCOLLECTED PROSE

ACKNOWLEDGEMENTS

We remember in particular Helen and Milton Singer. Milton was one of AKR's mentors. He was the prime mover behind AKR's appointment at the University of Chicago in 1962, and thirty-one years later, in finding a home for AKR's papers at the Regenstein Library, Chicago. He contacted Alice D. Schreyer, Curator, special collections, and concerned himself with details of the transfer of the manuscripts.

Helen, poet and friend, was an editor of *The Collected Poems*. Characteristically, she chose to remain unacknowledged; it was her habit to keep outside of history, and there is reason to believe that she threw her own poems in the incinerator the month before her death. This is as good a place as any to say that she would have been considered one of the recognized mid-century poets of this land had she published her book of poems. When she published in journals, she won prizes. Nine poems by Helen may be seen in *Poetry*. One could wish for no better elegy for AKR and for Milton and Helen Singer, Edward Shils, and S. Chandrasekhar, all friends of AKR's who died so close to each other, than the poem, 'A Good Man's Dying', by Helen Singer in *Poetry* (August 1959):

> It is the eyes that grieve
> In those who live by eyes
> Music cannot say
> What they would hear; but when they look
> They see the powdered leaves
> Of the autumn, and the impermanent

Buildings of the city
Looking everywhere, they expect to see the lost friend
In the image of his excellence

But then, those who live by hearing
Say they remember his voice
And no doubt those who were closer
And lived by his touch, recall that;
And are touched emptily by the warm docile air
Of this Indian Summer—

That like the legendary Indian Giver,
Both gives and takes away.

We thank Helen and Milton, and AKR's many friends who have contributed to the publication of his *Collected Poems, Collected Essays, The Flowering Tree* and this book. Grateful thanks are due to friends who are translating AKR's Kannada works into English, particularly Girish Karnad; to Mary Wallace, and Sharon Campbell Knox, and most of all to Maya Fisher, and Katherine E. Ulrich for editorial assistance, and to Norman Zidé for suggesting the inclusion of the interviews in the *Uncollected Poems*. James Nye, Bibliographer for Southern Asian Language and Area Center, at the University of Chicago, helped by solving a variety of problems related to bringing out four posthumous books. Last but not least, the editors thank Krittika Ramanujan for permission to use a reproduction of 'Poet in the Garden' which is from the artist's Dante Series. Everyone who helped prepare this book has been engaged by the poems, stirred by the interviews, dazzled by 'The Ring of Memory', and moved by the eulogy of Barbara Stoler Miller. We feel grateful to the 'legendary Indian Giver' for yet another A.K. Ramanujan volume.

Chicago, Illinois   Molly A. Daniels-Ramanujan
1995

PREFACE

—◆◆◆—

Even two years after his death, the grief and stupefaction felt by all of us who loved A.K. Ramanujan have lost none of their rawness. We are still reminded everyday of his absence. Yet there is something more poignant and even paradoxical about his loss and that is the persistent sense of his presence among us. He had, in a hundred ways, come to be a central person in our lives. His effect was that, in a subtle and quite un-programmatic way, he taught us a great deal of what we know about India, poetry, folklore, and much else. We carry him in our bones, in our minds' inner voice, in the ways we teach and read.

Reading through this volume brings that presence once again vividly alive. We hear that beautifully modulated voice, the sudden outburst of mirth, we admire the deftness and fastidiousness of his language. One thing, though, struck me much more forcefully than I had expected. Raman, as his friends called him, had never seemed to me a deeply political person in the sense that I could very easily have defined his place on the political spectrum: the day-to-day business of political events held little interest for him and he rarely spoke about them. Yet what emerges from this volume, and particularly from the interviews, is a vision of art and life which, if one can use the word in a much broader sense than usual, is deeply and consistently democratic. That needs some explaining.

When we look at what drew Raman to the early devotional poetry that he translated and collected in *Hymns for the Drowning*, when we consider the emphasis he gave throughout his work to the vernacular and regional literatures of India and elsewhere, I think we can see two major preoccupations. First, he was committed to the idea of poetry as an incarnation, perhaps (for him) the best incarnation of the spirit of a community. The second, which followed naturally, is that the dialects of regional communities had, for him, a freshness and particularity whose poetic possibilities and achievements were much more attractive than those of the colonizing and 'universal' Sanskrit and 'official' English. For him, the political allegory and the socio-linguistic theory embedded in Shakespeare's *The Tempest* were highly significant. Caliban learns English from Prospero but the result is that the island he once knew so intimately has, through the language of a distant, all-powerful monarch, become a place of exile.

My guess, though I never heard him speak about this directly, is that he would have claimed that such 'universal' languages, imported to places where they don't grow naturally, tend to produce a writing, a literature, and a culture which are to a large degree inauthentic. As an Australian 'brought up' on the language and culture of southern England, I can understand to some degree Raman's attitude towards the Sanskritic tradition in India, as well as to the more complex problem facing Indian writers who use English as their primary or even sole medium of composition. From his own trilingual experience, he was sharply aware of how language shapes and distorts the worlds we live in, how it can exclude as well as include, how the letter can kill. I believe it was this concern that drove him to work so long and devotedly on the non-Sanskritic sources in much that he undertook as a writer and scholar. It is something of the same impulse that sent William Carlos Williams running from Pound and Eliot and Europe in search of a poetry based on authentic American speech. The poet and critic, Karl Shapiro, once remarked that the only true American poets are Whitman and Williams. It was no accident that Raman was drawn to both.

It is for these reasons that, again and again, we find in the whole of Raman's life and work the figure of the bridge builder—in some senses that made him a paradox. He had all the poise and style of the Brahmin; yet he had the rare capacity of being 'ordinary'. He was by any account an outstanding figure. Though not without a certain vanity, for most of the time he wanted not to stand out but simply to be there, breathing, telling stories, cutting an orange, laughing outrageously, a person, an American, an Indian, both and neither. Just there.

This was Raman's essential genius, both as a person and as an artist. When he met you it was as if beneath all the chatter he was asserting one thing: I am your brother. There was nothing sentimental or self-conscious about this. It was as natural as a leaf unfolding. Yet hardly anyone who came into his presence failed to notice it and to feel an instant affinity. I forget who it was that said that the difficult thing is not the attaining of individuality, but arriving at the place where we understand that we are, in a profound way, all alike. Raman would have agreed. This is after all what, at root, the word 'kindness' implies. Raman's writing, teaching, and friendship were all acts of kindness.

This will, I hope, clarify what I meant earlier when I claimed that Raman's political temper was 'democratic'. It is something that is discernible throughout these poems and interviews, which constitute a valuable extended footnote to the work we already have. Just as he claimed that his translations consisted of three parts—the preface, the poems, and the afterword—which all worked in concert to 'translate the reader', these previously ungathered pieces work with all the rest in giving a more complete view of one of the outstanding literary humanists of our time.

If that view aspires towards completion, we must not forget something else, as what I have said so far can easily lead to a distortion. Beyond, or—to put it better—*included within* this Whitmanesque 'democratic' vision I have been speaking about, was something else. Raman also had a very pronounced dark side. I remember the first time I saw him at a distance I thought of an image I had seen somewhere of the brooding goddess Kālī. To make a leap, I have sometimes thought in reading his poems that his vision of the world is not all that far from Samuel Beckett and some of the other central modernists. Not long before his death he told me that he experienced almost every day an acute early morning depression which followed him well into his waking and working hours. One can only wonder whether his self-appointed task as a bridge builder, fulfilling commitments at many of the major universities in Europe and America, teaching and writing and chairing an academic department, was sometimes just too demanding. I had the sense that he was sometimes haunted by the feeling that, in all this activity, he did not have enough time to 'belong'.

But whatever the causes and characteristics of this more demonic side, the sketch I am giving here—'Raman the ordinary man' and 'Raman the keeper of the abyss'—is still a gross simplification. 'Think', he once challenged me, 'how many states of being, how many emotions you go through in the course of a single day. Who are you?' And, as he said it, he laughed mischievously.

So in these poems and interviews, as with all his work, we are left with someone who, like ourselves, is elusive. Yet, unlike ourselves, he had the wit and the courage to chart the river as it ran and as it carried him. Raman's thought was a delicate poise between a deep-rooted and grave skepticism and an even deeper belief in the essential goodness of the world. The tone of his mind is somewhat akin to that of Eliot's in *Ash Wednesday*. But there is something that marks him off sharply from Eliot, and it is signally important. Raman's poems, even at their darkest, do not invoke the terrible loneliness and isolation of Eliot. They always invite us to come in and share. They are emanations of a sane and joyful spirit, not unlike that of Feste in *Twelfth Night*. As I wrote at the time of his death, in a still uncompleted poem, the reason why his absence and his presence are still so strong upon us is that, for any who knew him, he has become our god of the hearth. But he is a god who is both companionable and completely human.

Keith Harrison
Carleton College,
Northfield, Minnesota
July 1995*

---

*The manuscript of this volume, prepared for publication in 1995, had to wait in line for three other posthumous works that have since been published.

UNCOLLECTED POEMS

Invisible Bodies

Turning the corner of the street
he found three newborn puppies
in a gutter with a mother curled
around them.

Turning the corner of the street
she found a newborn naked baby,
male, battered, dead in the manhole
with no mother around.

Turning the corner of the street
the boy stepped on the junkie
lying in the alley, covered with flies,
a dog sniffing his crotch.

Just any day, not only after a riot,
even among the gamboge maples of fall
streets are full of bodies, invisible
to the girl under the twirling parasol.

1951

1951. Village road in Dharwar.
A green snake crosses the road, curls down
from the tree on the left to the tree
in full flower, a gulmohur,
on the right.

Thin mouth line, black whip for a tongue,
triangle head lifted four inches high,
off-white underbelly
showing young bamboo nodes and he moves
in no hurry

at all from safety to danger to safety,
from camouflage in the green tree
to the dangers of being seen, stalked
by death waiting in a beak,
a boot or a stick,

or other futures in a wire cage
in a zoo, he moves on, five feet
from where I walked.

    Maybe a lesson there, but
    I don't learn it as I scurry
    from safety to safety, camouflage
    to camouflage in sun, shade, curtains
    of rain, newspapers,

    silences, tariffs, and window bars,
    cowering under the mythology
    of an imaginary sword
    hung by a horsehair over my head
    in sleep and waking.

Eagle and Butterfly

The eagle in the window
circles in and out of it
like an obsession

Butterflies zigzag from flower
to flower, settle on one, moving black
dots on orange wings very slowly

Uneasy with sentiments, brothers quarrel
about father's stamp collections
and mother's Persian carpets

Sing a song of sixpence, sing the twenty-four
blackbirds in my sleeping ears
waking me to childhood

Mother brings me tea again at 6 a.m.
before she dies in another time zone
and the calendar

whirls me out into snow flurries
and fears of market crash
in another hemisphere

*14 January 1992**

---

*Some of the poems have dates, and others do not; we abstained from adding anything to the text.

Twenty-four Senses

Hindus speak of twenty-four senses.
We have eyes and eyes behind eyes.
Skin sometimes can see lightnings,

eyebrows hear the snake's silence,
bare feet taste the moss in the pond.
Turning somersaults, the liver watches

the circulation of cells, the pancreas
open into a swirl of faces, the ovaries moving
in whalesongs in the middle of the Atlantic.

The thyroid feels the caress of the baby
at the breast, and the uterus goes into spasms
imagining fingers and toes not yet formed.

25 June 1991

Farewells

There are farewells
with formulae,
farewells
without.

At the railway
station, standing
at the window of your friend,
the train delayed
for two hours
and then again for another two,
you can neither go home
nor stop talking over and again
about the delay, the old days
when banana sellers were not rude
and tea was really from Darjeeling.

Also that recurring farewell
to the lady president
of the cooperative society
when they present her
with a silver medal
but don't have the time
to inscribe
her name.

So they take it back to get it
properly inscribed.
Now the secretary ducks
under his umbrella
and turns into the garbage alley
whenever he sees the lady
in the road
as he cannot bear the thought
of the unfinished farewell,
the nameless medallion
lost in his office drawer.

Then there is the farewell
of the dying patriarch
among all his clan:
the youngest grandson
standing next to grandpa
with the peculiar smell,
two mouths without front teeth,
mother crying into her sari, father busy on the phone
trying to locate brothers
on trains that do not arrive
according to the time changes in April.

> Mother's farewell had no words,
> no tears, only a long look
> that moved on your body
> from top to toe
> with the advice that you should
> not forget your oil bath
> every Tuesday
> when you go to America.

Figures of Disfigurement

Sick, disabled, twisting
through the bright days
the constable
of the market traffic
moves only his left hand
in sheer agony.
Men in cars, women on bikes
admire the grace of his movements.

Arthritic, the painter
makes new kinds of strokes
from his shoulder
keeping wrist and elbow rigid:
the exhibit of his latest pictures
opened yesterday.
The critics raved
about his technique.

The dyslexic suddenly
makes a reputation
deciphering a medieval diary,
a monk's secret life
written in code
that could be read
only by dyslexics
in a distorting mirror.

Epilepsy may confer
powers of ecstasy
sometimes; amnesia may
open memories of past
lives. Timely death
may give away a heart
or an eye.

13 January 1992

All Night

man in the street corner
yelling at his woman
sitting against a streetlight
knitting and saying nothing

all night lightnings lick
the sky like whipsnakes
and thunder rumbles
like garbage cans in the alley
but it doesn't rain

all night hands play
on bodies in several houses
heat wrings rivers of sweat
and it doesn't rain
it doesn't get dark

and it's grey
not even dark
between them

8 July 1991

Many a Slip

On Brothers' Day, sisters rescue brothers.
On Mothers' Day, sons worship mothers
who left them with babysitters
to go to movies. Resentment festers
on such days.

On New Year's Day, people make resolutions
to break them by evening: by four o'clock
they have quarrelled with their spouses,
watched the Rose Bowl soused on beer and nuts,
roused by the young

thighs of cheerleaders. Where do we go
from here? Why is Mars so far away?
Brothers and mothers written into the calendar,
time grows on the family tree and waves in the wind
like beards of Spanish

moss, shaking fingerbones as we look
for alligators in Florida keys.

Children, Dreams, Theorems

Children like dreams get lost
if they are not held close
caressed kissed named

dreams like poems get lost
if their tails are not knotted
for memory

poems like my father's midnight
theorems get lost if you do not
talk to them, take

their part in a quarrel
with their rival theorems
like dead languages

get lost if you do not smell them
early and change their diapers
sprinkle talcum on their bottoms

30 November 1991

However

however we say it
we're always wrong
when we say we can say it
right

when a daughter, a friend's
daughter falls in her bathroom
and dies, the body found
two days later

however we say it
we're always wrong
when we congratulate
a new acquaintance
on his recent wedding

and hear soon after
his wife's madness
flared up like a secret
basement fire
the day of the honeymoon

9 July 1991

Returning

Returning home one blazing afternoon,
he looked for his mother everywhere.
She wasn't in the kitchen, she wasn't
in the backyard, she wasn't anywhere.

He looked and looked, grew frantic,
looked even under the beds, where he found
old shoes and dustballs, but not his mother.
He ran out of the house, shouting, Amma!

Where are you? I'm home! I'm hungry!
But there was no answer, not even an echo
in the deserted street blazing with sunshine.
Suddenly he remembered he was now sixty-one

and he hadn't had a mother for forty years.

Anchors

Why is blue so blue and not turning green
as my moods do?

A haze of green as baby moss,
the brain's folds unfold
leaves in summer, walnut in a shell
longing for its mother tree,
fingers forming a hand not yet,
grasping at the corpuscles
in the amniotic sac,
the first word pressing towards
the last.

Depression weighs
an anchor in shallow waters,
the mud has forms of life.
I cannot talk to
ladies in white hats
around the swimming pool.

Chlorine blue,
depression stirs slow coils,
a python hungering for days,
stomach juices
eating its walls.

Girls turn into trees
in folktales.
Trees turn into girls
when I hug them,
at fourteen,
wanting that girl in the bus
sitting three rows out of reach
wafting smells of jasmine and sesame oil.

12 November 1991

On Julia

Eyes alternately blue, green, grey,
or brown as the lake.

Ears pink, whorls of sea shells
held up to the sun.

And so on.

Yet this beauty throws pots and pans
whenever she's in a rage.

Does not wake up till noon, does not
wash between her legs and her ruby lips

open only

to speak unspeakable obscenities.

Postmortem

She had shocked the plumber
who had found her
sitting on her toilet
seat in the living room
naked. She could not bear
the touch of clothes on her skin
in the last year of her life.

He had said, as he quickly
got out, his hand
on his head, 'Is that
what's going to happen
to us all?' Her downstairs
neighbour, in this casbah-like
warren of apartments,
was terrified
of her screams once a week
followed by long silences.

A statistician.
Lived alone with numbers
and graphs, a grey bun
on her spectacled head.
Numbers and graphs, not
even a cat.

Today her attorney
obedient to her wishes
was selling off her furniture,
pewter and Chinese soup bowls,
a TV and VCR for a few dollars each
and I had to hold back
from buying what I didn't need.
Still I bought a copper tray
and three rugs which I don't know
what to do with. Her body
went to Science, her attorney said,
the proceeds of her posthumous sale
would go to the University, her rugs
lie in my bedroom,
and where did the numbers go?

18 January 1992

Backstreet Visit

He put down cash, dollar bills,
before the pan-chewing madam
in the hills
and then he, and I
cowering deep within him, went
into the bare room
overcome
with the jasmine scent of a bed
under the bulb with a newspaper
cone for a shade.

The young woman, hardly a woman,
her voice a whisper of laryngitis,
asked him in her sibilant
language, maybe Thai, something
he didn't understand, then bent
double to peel off
her clothes, a brown
almond turning
her back to him
as I watched, down
to her panties

and bra that he was supposed to undo.
A kitten mewed in the next room.
She flinched.
I left in a hurry and he, he vanished
into my sweat and shudders.

29 March 1992

Smells

In certain rooms, he could still feel the print
of her presence—a hint of patchouli
perfume, a body odour of wet wood
and musk, and on his coat
a smell of Camels crushed:
                                        'Silly,' he said,
'She hasn't been here in three years, to the day.'

'But anniversaries are like that,' I say;
'I know men who panic at the thought
of turning fifty-seven on a Sunday
in December because their father died
at fifty-seven on a Sunday in December.
That's why we Hindus offer rice to crows
and to Brahmans, plain and speckled Vedic
toads heaving Sanskrit chants from their bellies
on ancestors' death days. The greedy way
they peck or guzzle on your rice
revives and feeds your hungry ancestors
ghosting it all this time, orphaned in reverse,
soundless cry-babies in the surrounding
air: Brahmans and crows, they make visible
the living dead, rousing and allaying
your anniversary fears.'

'Now what about this mix of cigarettes,
body musk and perfume, every year
this day, in this new room, swept and washed
and dusted every two days?'
                                        'Buy your wife,'
I say, acting wise and wicked, 'patchouli
perfume, then smoke only Camels, wet that
firewood in your verandah, and don't mind
the difference in body odours.'

8 December 1992, Hyderabad
11 April 1993.

Love 10

Love poems, he says, are not easy to write
because they've all been written before.
Words play dead. The seasons are trite.

Love poems are not easy to write
for anyone present: their lips are sore,
hearts elsewhere, or just full of spite.

And love poems are not easy to write
for absent ones: can't remember any more
the colour of their eyes, try as one might.

Love poems are not easy to write
for the dead: after the sting of sorrow,
ironies of relief, one's stricken with blight.

Turning over and over tomorrow
and yesterday, day is already night.
Love, unwritten, cataracts his sight.

Time Changes

Time changes on the clocks each day.
Friction in the wheels, fuses blown,
other watches offering corrections,
plane trips to a different time zone,

even a lack of graphite, a ray
of sunshine on a solar plate,
some people say your own heart rate
can change time on the clocks you trust.

Yet nothing changes time like dust
and ashes in the mouth after love
on the beach in the afternoon bay

either because you'd had enough
or your lover saw your past
in her future writ large on the day.

Museum

As people who appear in dreams
are not themselves, the horses
are not horses in the Chinese painting
that prance out of the walls
to trample the flowers
in the emperor's gardens
night after night.

Those children on the swing
are your childhood;
old men the ageing cells,
portraits of Spinoza and Confucius
wisdom of the hardening
artery, ancestors of family joke
and legend in the faded sepia
photographs on the puja wall.

Flowers are inward vaginal
Georgia O'Keefe spirals
not darkening but swathed
in more and more light
as they deepen.

Or erect male stamens
dotted moist with yellow
pollen ready to seed your eye
mouth ear nostril
reeking with lowtide smells
even as you watch
in the white museum
with guards in navy blue
uniforms.

A Rationalist Abroad

Placing your hand on a ouija board,

it's like dipping into a river underground
that's always flowing.

Slicing a piece of living flesh for the slip
under the microscope.

Stopping in the middle of the market to look
what's happening in your mind.

Hunting for the aphrodisiac rhino in the Himalayas
and finding the blue spears of winter flowers.

Counting the pulse of a flying sparrow
flying alongside of it.

Placing your hand on the ouija board and writing
the maiden name of your mother that no one knew.

Daily Drivel: a monologue

I cannot tell you how many things I did
in the four hours you were gone:
showed my burning bottom to a young doctor
who inevitably had to finger me deep
and palpate my prostate;
hobbled back to do my laundry,
huff and puff at my weights at the gym,
run in the rain to the grocery store
for lettuce and the forbidden ice cream,
get my income tax returns postmarked
by a surly post office,
eat my dinner of spinach, pasta, and yoghurt,
and send off taxi receipts to a college
where I'd lectured two days ago,
and write this daily drivel
which I hadn't done for a week.
I even washed all my cups and saucers,
and put away my forks and spoons
in the drawer, and sat down for ten whole minutes
doing nothing. But you went
singlemindedly to see Othello,
deepening your sense of life,
while I scattered my hours
on the wind not even wishing
they were precious seed
that could sprout a harvest
by springtime.

15 April 1992

Lying

When the patient has cancer,
they tell him: Patience
is the answer, it's a boil
that will heal.

When the mother died,
the daughter said
she gave her all the jewellery,
and tore the gold from every side.

He told the dead Indian
at Wounded Knee, he would make
reparations in Congress.

She told the man in her bed,
he was the best lover she'd ever had,
and he told her she was beautiful.
All his life her bastard son wet his bed.

The father told the boy
his incontinent dog was going
to the hospital,
not to the animal shelter
to be put to sleep.

He told himself he would never
again ask his father for money,
on his way to his apartment
to ask him to pay his car insurance
this one time.

Turning around, he prayed to his god,
saying he'd like to see him:
all he wanted was to be able to say
to everyone he's seen Him,
so he could start an ashram.

The newborn was ugly, moist,
hairy all over like a wet rat:
every visitor said
she was a beauty,
had her mother's eyes.

11 October 1992

Waiting

Waiting for a friend from Milwaukee
to pick me up on Sunday
I looked out the window.
A family of four, young bearded father,
tall mother slim in white shorts,
son practising imaginary baseball
on the sidewalk as he walks ahead,
and daughter, small and busy, trying
cartwheels on the strip of new grass
between sidewalk and the car-
ridden road. They were waiting
for nothing, while I waited, as always
for someone to arrive from somewhere
and take me somewhere else.
As I watched them
turn into 57th street, I too waited
for nothing for a moment.

Bluebottles

Purple lightnings streak the sky
with momentary forks and branches
the day father died and mother
wanted to die with him.

When crocuses poke their mauves
and yellows through the snow
in slums dying of dysentery
I've seen children with runny noses
watch them, touch them, look at them closely.

Bluebottles zing about on the garbage
heap, glinting in multiple colours.

27 March 1992

Dances Remember Dancers

Questions cling to answers.
Why did LA burn the day
his girlfriend died?

Dances remember dancers.
As she lay dying in May,
her feet moved like the tide.

The body was not hers,
yet a ray of light on the bay
sent her heart on a ride.

Fingers rang for the nurse
and he heard her say,
You lied, you lied!

This disease is a curse,
the month is already May
and I haven't yet died.
Dances remember dancers
when they can't tell day
from night, mother from bride.

6 May 1993

Suddenly

money and pity do not cure
the pang, milk and Tagore
no longer fill the hollow,
wife and child once candy-sweet
sink bitter root in the tongue
as night broods on the eggs
of day.

> The rummaging poor
> in the garbage alley
> even in distant Salvador
> come close, arms and legs
> seem too little
> to give away and money
> festers in the bank,
> a sore dipped in a septic tank.

30 May 1992

Surviving*

In Auschwitz time stopped
like menstrual cycles.
One man lived for a bowl
of bean soup with a fish head
looking at him almost
with affection.

Another looked for a fleck
of sun on a spear of grass
during morning roll call
as a woman for the pleasure
of a bowel movement
smelling of asparagus.

White 'milliseconds of sanity
in a long red madness',
a minute's rest on the roadside
breaking stones, a man
in the next bed reciting
in rhyme a recipe for soufflé.

*Details from Des Pres' *The Survivor*

Becoming

On the grass of sloping hills
a scatter of white sheep,
unravelling already like the balls
of wool they are going to be.

Snake and iguana sleep in the sun
looking already polished
like women's wallets and gigolo
shoes, yet afraid of cats and hawks.

Deer and doe run on the desert
sand, dry, off-white as the backs
of deerskins for gurus
to sit on, or for secular

living rooms. Men and women run
races in faraway places like Seoul
and Munich, make four-minute miles,
beat their own records, to become videos

and photographs that sell shoes.

Computers Eat Fingertips

computers eat fingertips
spears of asparagus
and begin to hear
a wife's mother say
she was plucked out of the ground
by her ears a pair of cabbage leaves
around a head of cabbage
her brother says
he was not born but bought at the door
from a gypsy for a measure of rice
children grow up twining creepers
around an oak twisted and dying
of the parasitic embrace of suckers
blue jays flash through the sunlit porch
looking for peanuts they don't have to shell
the husband in an easy chair
shelling peanuts watching the oak twist
under the talons of creepers thinking
of cabbage leaves his wife's mother's fingers
like yellow lizards her thoughts
stuck in biblical olive trees
gypsies hungering for a mouthful of rice
computers make and eat words at fingertips
spewing out wife brother mother husband
easy chair oak gypsies rice
munching on a mouthful of asparagus

1 December 1991

He to Me or Me to Him*

when I was translating
twenty years ago
the saints who sang
ten centuries ago about Śiva
without any thought of me

I didn't have any
thought of a young man
in Madras ten years ago
who would read them

through my words
night and day
his hand toying with pills
his eyes with colours
turning on a wheel

swallowing them
with the poems
that had no thought
of him or me who had

no thought of him
gasping in the mist
between day and the needles
in the wrist between
to be or not to be

---

*I was translating last week the Tamil poems of Ātmānām. He had attempted suicide in
1983. I thought he was the best of the poets in Tamil. While I was translating, it occurred
to me to read the biographical note at the end of the book. To my shock, I read there
that he was reading night and day my Speaking of Śiva just before he attempted suicide.
I had some connection with him that I couldn't quite define.

leaving behind poems
for me to read
and to translate this week
without a thought
of him who had thought

of me and the saints
who spoke through me
to him yet had told him
nothing nothing at all

26 November 1991

Renoir at Eighty

when a painter's fingers
are fixed in arthritis
the lines change

a marathon runner's feet
shackled in an Achilles' heel
he becomes an angry coach

an accountant's brain tumour
makes numbers dance
and honesty flicker

beauty like Rita's grows
grey in Alzheimer's
needs a toilet in the living room

yet Renoir ties a brush
to his frozen fingers
and paints at eighty

30 November 1991

Oranges

Oranges on the refrigerator
are covered with the ash of living
mould that would look like a sci-fi
undersea forest through a microscope.

The woodpile in the backyard twinkles
with green-eyed bacteria
even through January snows
that blanket and put everything

to sleep except waiting crocuses,
bears and children unwilling
to grow beyond Christmas Eve.

Snows feed the springs of summer.
Bacteria thrive in the kissing mouth,
the dying brain. Just wait,

you too will live again.

TWO INTERVIEWS

INTERVIEW ONE

———◆◆◆◆◆———

Chirantan Kulshrestha was 24 and A.K. Ramanujan 41 at the time of their first meeting; they met again ten years later. The following interview was in the main conducted in 1970, at the University of Chicago, during Kulshrestha's Fulbright year. He returned to Chicago ten years later as a visiting Fellow of the American Council of Learned Societies and the Andrew Mellon Foundation. Kulshrestha was by then author of *Saul Bellow: The Problem of Affirmation* (1978). Soon after his year-long second visit to Chicago, he died of bone cancer, in December 1982.

CK: It seems to me that the fact of your writing poetry in English in America raises certain interesting questions about your attitude as a poet to the audiences of two different cultural milieus. On the one hand, you belong to a representative group of Indian writers who have chosen English as a medium of their art and produced a body of writing with a colour and character all its own. In a way you are part of this group and these writers are your compeers. On the other hand, you have lived in America a long time, have published here, and to identify you exclusively with the Indo-Anglians seems a little far-fetched. In this sense your real compeers are contemporary American poets, since very probably you are not unaware of the experiments they are conducting in their techniques, and even unconsciously their work affects your orientation as a poet. I would like to know how you react to this situation.

AKR: Opinions are only a small expression of one's attitudes. They are an uncertain, often rigid expression. One is more, and often less, than one's opinions. And they don't often match other things in oneself. So please read them as gestures.

Now to your question: You speak of 'Indian writers who have chosen English'. The language of one's writing is not a matter of *choice*. Poems don't come to you abstractly and then you ask: 'Shall I write in Tamil, English, or Kannada? Which is the best language for this?' I think a lot of the controversy about Indian writing in English is mistaken. Some Indians wish to write in English and others accuse them of writing in English; both of them seem to believe there is a choice in the matter. The question is not whether you wish to write or not, but whether you can. If you can, you will. And if you do, you must be judged by results.

Why do I write in English? Many reasons—none of them literary. The simplest and most mentionable are (a) my long years of education in English and (b) having lived away from my first-language areas for nearly twenty years, making English my chief language of conversation with my peers and even my family. Though by a curious perversity I read Tamil constantly in the Kannada area, Kannada in the Tamil area, studied and taught English in India, and India and Indian languages in the US. Such perversity, I suppose, serves to keep alive the immediately absent parts of me.

I had a Kannada poet friend in Chicago for a few months and we talked Kannada endlessly through the winter snows and the TV shows of Apollo 2. Strangely enough at the end of two or three months of it, I started spouting Kannada poems. I wrote more feverishly, poured out more 'poems' in a short time than I have ever done before.

CK: Now, because the selection of the medium of your poetry is not really a matter of choice but a certain kind of inner compulsion, would it mean that you were not confronted with the problem an Indian writing in English is usually confronted with—the problem of conveying a certain native sensibility in a foreign language because of the differences in nuances?

AKR: The language of a poem is not a matter of conscious problem solving and New Year's Day resolutions. If you have a problem, it shows in your work. No amount of *thinking* about grammar and idiom can resolve these problems because you are not *putting together* a composition. You are actively composing—or decomposing. Indians writing in English are mostly writing in a second language, and it raises several questions. A second language clearly has disadvantages for a writer—some of them disastrous. To enumerate a few: Usually a second language is not learned in childhood. When one writes in a second language not learned in childhood, superimposed on a first, one may effectively cut oneself off from one's childhood. A great deal of what we are in life and in writing goes back to that period when language was being formed inside, forming us, forming the world of concepts, the style of our perceptions. No man can deny or insulate that source of his sensibility without peril. Second languages also tend to be learned formally. They are not learned or used in an active community of native speakers, though it may be somewhat different for a few city Indians. It's true, that a great deal of live intellectual dialogue in south Indian cities does take place in English still. But few of us know English well enough to describe common intimate things in English—a kitchen operation, an obscure gesture, a family quarrel. We're split linguistically in so many ways. In our house, for instance, we spoke Kannada outside, and Tamil downstairs. Indoors/outdoors, child/adult, library/bedroom cut through us, don't they? Anyone using English may often use it only as an upstairs idiom and use his mother tongue downstairs. This kind of split is disastrous for a poet. This doesn't of course mean that poets in first languages may not suffer similar splits. Classical Sanskrit poets must have suffered similar splits. Bad writing is not the monopoly of Indian writers.

CK: How did you escape it?

AKR: Thanks, but I don't know if I've escaped it. A great deal of Indian writing is upstairs English, platform English, idiom-book English, newspaper English. With no slang available, they are stuck in a 'register', a formality, a learned posture. It often reminds me of certain deep sea fish that can only live in a narrow band adapted to a certain depth, they can go neither up nor down—and if by chance they are thrown up to the surface, they burst their bellies—they can't stand the change in pressure. A second language speaker often speaks and spells much more correctly than a first language speaker—see the errors in Keats' or Yeats' letters. Such 'rectified language' isn't always a good thing for a creative writer. One of the articles in a recent *Indian Literature* issue says this situation has changed in recent Indian English poetry. I don't see the change. Nothing like the efforts of Raja Rao in *Kanthapura* to write a Kannada English, or of Desani in *Hatterr* to write a full-blooded comic Indian English, has happened in Indian English verse. Even those two efforts haven't stuck; they were successful freaks. First-rate, especially Desani—yet, a freak.

CK: You think the Indian English poet is correct, in a stiff-necked sense.

AKR: The starch is always showing on the collar. He can't be carefree, unruly. He's always asking himself, 'Dare I eat a peach?' and he dare not bite into it. Not that some poetry cannot be written that way; I'm sure some poetry can be written in any register. But it's bound to be limited. Most of us who for some reason or other write in English have probably written ourselves into the margin, because of such splits in our persons and in our language. And they are big splits. With a foreign second language like English, we also get separated from the great community of people in India. We become dependent on cliques and coffee-house 'elites'.

But then, a person does not write simply out of the present. If he's worth the ink, he writes with everything he is. What you write not only expresses you, it betrays you; you risk judgement at every hand. Yet some people are other people, and cannot be themselves. There's no other way, except to be oneself in the language one uses, even in the second language, to find a voice which is one's own, however cracked or small, sick or normal, which follows one's twists and turns, falls and rises and stumbles, in one's 'climb to one's proper dark'—though the climb may be like a monkey's on a greased pole, two feet up and three feet down. I don't know how one does it. If only one can be in touch with this level of the linguistic unconscious, this wholeness. True language use is unconscious in this sense; the more self-conscious it is, the more artificial it becomes, and the more trammelled in manners, rules, opinions. Maybe it's by vigilantly negating what is not yourself that you finally find some place in your language (and your world) where you do not have to mimic and perform, like Johnson's women orators and dancing dogs. Not that dog dances and flea circuses don't begin to be expressive somewhere—nor that they don't have their bizarre uses and charms.

CK: While we are at it, let me go back to your own poetic process, to what you said about talking Kannada through the snows and 'spouting' poems afterwards. How do poems come to you? What roles do you assign to inspiration, feeling, and craft?

AKR: I don't really know. Poems come in different ways. Sometimes I work on a poem for 10 years—not that it makes the poem any better—it may ripen or just rot, crabbed beyond recovery. I do rework poems a lot. Something around me often touches me and returns me to an old unfinished piece and makes me see what I tried to say there. I return to it and redo it and if this redoing is any good, it reflects not only the change in myself, but in redoing it I find myself changed. So there is a kind of dialectic between oneself and the poem one is writing. Inspiration is not only at the beginning of poems and things; the craft has to be inspired continually. Every little change, every self-criticism you make has to be a creative act. There is no line between craft and inspiration, no real line between intelligence and imagination. At that point it's sensibility (I almost said 'character') or nothing—all through, in the beginning, the middle, the end. If not, it'll really show. There'll be dead words, holes, borrowings, helpless patches, betrayals.

CK: And looking at the poems published long ago, do you feel like doing more to them?

AKR: Some of them, yes, certainly. Valery said, a poem is really never finished, it is only abandoned. By printing it you put a kind of moratorium on it. Why only poems—nothing is really truly finished. Reminds me of the *Punch* cartoon, of a bewildered man at a desk writing his autobiography, agonizingly asking himself: 'How shall I end it?' I do the translations in the same way. I began the translation of Kannada *vacanas* in 1952. It will be published in 1972.

CK: While recently reading your translations of Tamil love poems and comparing their vividly imagistic and compressed quality with that of your own poems in *The Striders*, I had the feeling that at the base somewhere there was an affinity at work. Am I right in supposing this? And if such an affinity exists, what is its nature? Also, what were the reasons behind your choice of the form of the short poem in *The Striders*?

AKR: These classical Tamil poems attracted me by their attitude to experience, to human passion, and to the external world; their trust in the bareness, the lean line with no need to jazz it up or ornament it. They seemed to me Classical, anti-Romantic, using the words loosely as we know them in European literature. A great deal of modern Indian writing has been ruined by Romanticism of the Shelleyan variety. And not just our writing but our taste (both in Indian languages and in English). We have been recovering from it in this generation. Look at the classical Tamil poems, their attention to experience. Yet their attention to the object is not to create the 'object' of the Imagist, but the object as enacting human experience: the scene always a part of the human scene, the poetry of objects always a part of the human perception of self and others.

This seemed to me an extraordinary way of writing poetry. I came upon these first-century poems in Chicago. I started reading them hesitantly, not being formally trained in classical Tamil. I was amazed at the transparency of the poems, the sophistication of the early commentators. And so I acquired some facility in reading them by teaching nothing else for some time. My training as a linguist and my experience as a native Tamil speaker surely were a help. When I started translating them, I found that there were any number of poems which I would have liked to have written myself. I do not translate out of love but out of envy, out of a kind of aggression towards these great poems. I think one translates out of a need to appropriate someone else's creation, done better than one could ever do. The ability to engage entirely the world of things, animals, trees, and people, attending to their particularity, making poetry out of it and making them speak for you—this seems to me extraordinary.

There were also the obvious contrasts between the classical Tamils and people like me, belonging to no group or tradition, not schooled or groomed for any. Any number of mixtures go into this hopper that one calls oneself. From the almost random 'rag-and-bone shop' of the heart, one falls or 'climbs to one's proper dark'. But the ancient Tamils were a community, a 'Sangam' of poets, with a symbolism and a reality they shared. Not a fabulous mythology, but the realities of nature and culture used as a symbolism, a language within a language which allowed them to write with tremendous economy and allusiveness. Describe a drumbeat or falling water or a wildcat's row of teeth; one little thing could say many things. If the world was the vocabulary of the poet, convention was his syntax. And this was truly matter for envy.

In India today we do share, entirely unawares, a great stock of symbolism and mythology. Most of us writing in English don't use it. We filter it out, because we wish to write English English. Self-conscious, we write out of a corner of ourselves filtering out our childhood, our obscenities, our bodies, our mythologies, the rich fabric of allusion that a first language is. (Many first language poets are no better; they do the same.) You don't just write with a language, you write with all you have. When I write in Kannada, I'd *like* all my English, Tamil, etc. to be at the back of it; and when I write in English I *hope* my Tamil and my Kannada, like my linguistics and anthropology, what I know of America and India, are at the back of it. It's of course only a hope, not a claim. I'm less and less embarrassed or afraid of keeping all of these doors open even when it's dark outside and it's 3 a.m. inside.

You ask me about the short poems. Those were written much before I was acquainted with these Tamil poems. But I've always had need for conciseness, like the Frenchman who wrote a twenty-page letter, with a postscript at the end: 'If only I had more time I could have written a shorter letter.' Part of the pleasure, the power, of poetry lies in the fact that it can condense, speak through a near-silence, make words say more than words can tell. Such density is dear to me. As you know, this is nothing new to either Tamil or Sanskrit.

CK: The qualities of verse I mentioned in the last question seem to have stayed in *Relations,* though the tone seems to have become more mature (shall I say ancient?) and quizzical. There is even an attempt to write longer poems. How would you describe your change of attitude during the six years that span *The Striders* and *Relations*?

AKR: For one thing, almost all the *Striders* poems were written before 1964. Since then I've been doing translations, deepening my acquaintance with the Indian, especially the classical Tamil and medieval *bhakti*, traditions. These traditions explore character and relationships in a lyrical, not a novelistic, way; and include, imply, a great human scene; they create a world through sequences of interacting poems.

I have tried to keep the human scene central in the poems. The more I pay attention to the human world, for me the line between the poem and the novel, the lyric and the story, begins to blur; and anyway in Indian poetry there's never been a clear line. Any single poem implies a persona, a voice, a specific scene, a whole dramatic situation. This is true of both the Tamil poems and the Sanskrit ones.

CK: And the long poems?

AKR: I had rather held myself too narrowly in *The Striders*. Some of the poems didn't move freely. So I have been feeling my way towards a longer stanza, a looser line, tones of greater range.

CK: I have a reservation about the longer poems you have been attempting in *Relations*. Although you say that you were prompted to write longer poems because you were not content just with the density and precision of the short poems, it seems to me that sometimes your longer poems create the appearance of being a cluster of short poems strung together. So the condensation *is* there; all that has happened is that a couple of short pieces have been put together to form a larger—shall I say expanded—movement.

AKR: There are two kinds of poems there of this sort; one is a sequence of poems, variations on a theme, as in a sonnet cycle. If a thing is important to you, it becomes an obsession. Actually, that's what you mean by saying it's important to you. If it's obsessive you begin to see it everywhere for a while and soon find you have written several poems on the same theme, though you might have given it different names; often these poems take similar forms, share a vocabulary, a repertory of symbols, voices. Gradually a number of poems gather around a single obsession often in a progression, a sequence. There are about three or four such sequences in the new book: 'Sample Entries in a Catalogue of Fears'; a series of prayers to Lord Murugan, the ancient Dravidian god; and one on the modern Indian's uses of history, both honest and dishonest.

CK: I also find very striking the use you make of memory in your poetry: in *Relations* it even significantly affects the tone and the form of your poems, and seems to have become, at the same time, an important vehicle of communication as well as an effective mode of experimentation. What special meaning does memory have for you and in what way does it enter the writing of your verse?

AKR: I don't really know. I simply write poems as they occur to me; I have to have no theory. It is true I have a number of poems which are obsessed not only with memories but with memory itself, memory as history and myth, memory as one's own past—the presence of the past—the way the present gathers to itself different pasts. This kind of concern can, of course, lead to the no-more and the have-been and the not-yet all weaving into and out of the here-and-now. You have to find a way of bringing all these together and still not confuse or diffuse the form of the work. But this is nothing new.

CK: Do you propose to make experiments in other poetic forms, even other literary genres?

AKR: I do not plot and propose experiments, though some pages do. Each poem has to find its form and, in finding its form, it has to be 'an experiment'. In finding this form, one often uses models, precedents, traditions, re-shaping them in one way or another. As the proverb has it: one may count the number of oranges in a tree, not the number of trees in an orange. If you look at my stanzas or sonnets, you'll see I make up new kinds as I go along. As I change, I hope my expression too will change. Regarding the future, after having written a poem there is always a question, a fear whether you will ever write another. Other poets have spoken of this. I'm a little superstitious about that. I don't know how or when or why one writes a poem. If I may read an old poem (from *The Striders*) into this exchange:

Which Reminds Me

> I have known
> that measly-looking man,
> not very likeable, going to the bank
> after the dentist,
> catching a cold
> at the turn of the street
> sitting at the window of the local bus,
> suddenly make
> (between three crossings and the old
> woman at the red light)
> a poem.
>
> Which reminds me
> of the thrown-away seed
> of the folktale tree
> filling with child the mangy palace dog
> under the window,
> leaving the whole royal harem
> barren.

I don't really have any plans: I hope simply to drift into another poem and still another. I do my translations meanwhile—have just finished translating Anantha Murthy's novel *Saṃskāra*. I'm continuing work on my larger volume of classical Tamil poems. I began with plays originally and hope some day to do some.

CK: How do you view contemporary Indian poetry in English?

AKR: I am not a critic. Contemporary Indian poetry in English has come in for a lot of fruitless attack and defence: it needs neither. What it needs is a good critic—it has now only log-rolling cliques, patrons, and enemies. And academics. Indian writing in English is one of several bodies of live writing in India—though it gets more attention than it deserves at present, chiefly because it's the only Indian writing that most foreigners can read at first-hand.

It is also good to promote it, as do men like P. Lal who not only writes and translates but helps fellow writers in every way. Many of us owe much to the friendship of P. Lal and Nissim Ezekiel. Yet as editors I wish they would heed what an ancient Tamil poet once said to his patron:

> Pari! Pari! they cry,
> these poets
> with their good red tongues
> praising one man
> in many ways:
>> yet it's not only Pari,
>> the rains too
>> keep the world
>> going
>> in these parts.

It is very much in the Indian tradition to write in a second language. When Kālidāsa wrote his best classical Sanskrit poems I'm sure he didn't speak Sanskrit at home as first language or mother tongue. He probably spoke some rather far-out dialect related to Sanskrit, but certainly not the 'high' Sanskrit he wrote. And later when the Persian tradition came to India, people wrote *ghazals* and *masnavis* in Persian. It's not unusual that a small group of people in a country should express themselves in a second language that they have internalized sufficiently to write in, to speak in, to conduct their affairs in, Mr Lal would say 'to make love in'—though I don't know if you make love in languages. Further, compare it with the writing in the languages—such comparisons are frequently used to beat Indian English writing with. If you take the number of stillborn poems, I don't think the rate is higher than in the regional languages. If you take the higher ranges, i.e. the better writers, I think the language writers have greater density, greater range. There is nobody like Tagore or Bose or Karanth or Masti or Adiga or La Sa Ra or Karnad writing in English; either in intensity, output, variety, creative use of our past and present, or power of influence. But on the other hand, if you look at the middle standard—a kind of general competence in writing—I think there are proportionately more competent second-rate writers in English than in the languages.

The purely statistical claim that people are always making is that more English is being used for articulatory purposes in India. It spans all the regions of India, as Sanskrit once did; more books, newspapers, etc. are being printed in English, and so on. I think that may not be so relevant. It has more to do with market research than the quality of writing, though it might affect the quality of a writer's food.

INTERVIEW TWO

———— ✦ ————

A.L. Becker and Keith Taylor interviewed AKR at the University of Michigan in 1989, while he was on the faculty there. A.L. Becker is Professor Emeritus of Linguistics at the University of Michigan. His most recent book is *Beyond Translation* (University of Michigan Press, 1995). Keith Taylor is author of a chapbook of poetry and of *Life Science: A Collection of Short Stories*. He manages an academic bookshop in Ann Arbor and teaches at the University of Michigan.

KT: There has been a good deal of discussion recently about the condition of the modern writer or thinker as being a condition of exile. Much of your work points towards this condition. Do you consider yourself an exile?

AKR: No. An exile is a person who has been thrown out of his country. I'm not one. I have come to this country voluntarily. If you're thinking of an exile as someone who has lived in another country or another culture, and suffers from the discomforts, possibly also the impoverishment of living in another culture, there are lots of dislocations. I don't think that should be called exile. Where people have moved voluntarily to get jobs or education or to live more comfortably, 'exile' would be too sentimental a term.

I don't even call myself an expatriate, because I've done a lot of work on India since coming to this country. I've done it more comfortably here than I could even have done it in India. For instance, in the Chicago Regenstein Library, there are books in Kannada and Tamil which probably only I will read. It's a great library that is more or less only for a couple of people like me. When I went to Delhi—I was working on some classical Tamil poems—I had to go for miles to find a classical Tamil book.

And the other interesting thing is that one can be an internal alien in India, as one goes from one province to another. I have not lived in my own language region since my 20th year. If you go a hundred miles away, you are in a language that you cannot read or speak.

KT: You left for more education?

AKR: No. I finished my education at 20, and then went to work. I travelled from place to place for about seven years, teaching English.

Also, being an educated Indian today, you are inevitably bicultural. You are educated in English, and you have your mother tongue. Someone like me has two mother tongues: the childhood languages in addition to English. So you are, in various ways and from childhood on, exposed to more than one culture. I have literally lived my life in three different cultures, although they are connected.

I think it is in the dialogue of these three cultures—which I sometimes refer to as downstairs, upstairs, and outside the house—and in the conflict between these three languages, that I am made. That's not special to me. About 10 percent of India is bilingual. If they happen to be educated, they will be trilingual.

KT: Let me see if I have the metaphor right. The downstairs language would be Tamil?

AKR: Tamil. Yes. The language of my family. Kannada would be the language of the city, Mysore. The language outside the house. English would be upstairs.

ALB: Upstairs would be the father?

AKR: Yes. I sometimes call them father tongues and mother tongues. My father was a mathematician. He did much of his work in English, and he literally lived upstairs. His library was there.

KT: Did you receive religious education in Sanskrit?

AKR: No. My father tried. But he himself was not a very religious man. He knew Sanskrit well, and he recited the *Gītā*, read the

Rāmāyaṇa in the morning, as his ancestors had done. But he was sporadic in his prayers. He was an in-between man about it.

I did a piece once in India that began with a description of my father. Both in his clothes and in his intellectual life, he was both Indian and European. In his mathematics, he would just as easily talk about the old Sanskrit texts as he would about Leibniz or Euclid or non-Euclidian geometry. He was an astronomer of some note. At the same time, he was also an astrologer.

This used to bother me a lot. 'How can you do this?' I would ask him. We used to have a lot of arguments about this when I was 16 or 17.

KT: Did your father have a western education?

AKR: Yes. But he never went to Britain. He published in Britain a lot. And America.

ALB: Which part of this life did you share? Was it the religion? The prayers? The astrology?

AKR: No. I was very much against astrology. I said astronomy was good, but astrology—throw it away.

ALB: But what did you do with your father?

AKR: Astronomy. A lot. All the things that were acceptable to me. I never shared with him the other things. When he would cast horoscopes and things like that, I would dismiss them. I said things to him that were quite insulting.

ALB: Did it bother him?

AKR: Oh, yes. He would argue with me. I would say to him, 'Now that Pluto and Neptune have been found, how can your seven planet astrology work?' He would say, 'You don't know about mathematicians. We make the necessary corrections'.

He would just as easily talk about atheism and Bertrand Russell as he would about the *Bhagavad Gītā*. Quite early he had said to me, 'Don't you know that there are two lobes to the brain?'

I became convinced as I got older that he needed two worlds emotionally. He needed them for imaginative reasons.

He would be rationalistic. But he knew that mathematics, Pythagoras and all that, came out of all kinds of astrological investigation.

He was sophisticated enough to come back at me. The Pythagorean theories, both in India and in Greece, were responses to various kinds of ritual. When the Delphic Oracle told them to double the altar, they first multiplied it by two and it didn't work. Then they reinterpreted the notion of doubling as squaring. My father gave me a very similar reason for why the Indians developed square root. The same kind of thing is in the Śulva Sūtras, which are about altar making. My father was giving me reasons why ritual and religion are all involved in the sciences. Only modern science has lost all that. And even there one can't be certain.

KT: Was your reaction at 16 a reaction against India?

AKR: Against Hinduism. And, of course, I had the notion that only a kind of modern rationalism was the answer to all the problems that we had: the caste system, the problems of a hierarchy by birth. It seemed to me then, it still does, as unfair. That is true of many modern Indians. The more political persons would have an even stronger reaction to it.

KT: Yet much of your professional life as translator or as folklorist has been a very sympathetic portrayal of religious life.

AKR: Yes. But even there you will find that my interest, my unconscious agenda, has been to diversify our notions of Indian civilization. To take it away from the purely Brahmanical view of Indian civilization. The Brahmanical view is a hierarchical one. If you look at something like *Speaking of Śiva*, you find it more democratic. It is fiercely critical of Hindu positions of ritual and priests, the privilege of temples, and the rich men who support the temples—of the whole caste system.

I have never translated the Vedas. My interest has always been in the mother tongues, not Sanskrit, because I have always felt that the mother tongues represent a democratic, anti-hierarchic, from-the-ground-up view of India. And my interest in folklore has also been shaped by that. I see in these counter-systems, anti-structures, a protest against official systems.

My work in folklore represents the world of women and children. More or less unconsciously, I have decided not to talk about India through the Sanskrit texts, but through the mother tongue texts, both written and oral. India not as seen through some epic like the *Rāmāyaṇa*, which privileges the male, but through folk epics, folk tales which are told by women, by the non-literate part of the population. This has been my preoccupation.

KT: What are the simple logistics of finding these folktales? Do you collect them yourself? Do you find them written in the mother tongues?

AKR: First of all, I came upon these tales because they were told at home by grandmothers, by cooks. For instance, when we were young, all the children of the house would be brought together in the kitchen and made to sit in a circle. If there was a grandmother or an older woman in the house, she would mix the food, and give it in small morsels—literally morsels, meaning bites—to each of the children. The child would put out her hand or his hand, and the woman would put the food in the hand. While we were eating, we would get a tale, basically to make us forget that we were eating. Tales in south India, in the kind of family I grew up in, were not bedtime stories but foodtime stories.

I often say that these tales demonstrate a grandmotherly love. Rarely does a mother tell these stories. So there is no power relation. The grandmother or cook or aunt tells the story, and the usual power relation in the family is cancelled.

KT: Is there a standard repertoire of these tales?

AKR: Yes. There are lots of them. Thousands, maybe. It's usually evening when the child is somewhat tired. And it's connected with food. So food, sleep, and love—what can be more hypnotic? That's why I think they're very formative. That was my other interest in the folktales. I felt that they were told early enough to children to be important.

There are three things in which I'm constantly interested—the aesthetics, the past, and the world view. All three of them are important in these tales, even more in these tales than in the mythologies. In the mythologies, one hears the official views.

KT: Is there a quick example of one of these grandmother tales?

AKR: Here's one. It's a story about stories. It's about a woman who knew a story and a song, but she would never tell them.

One day the story and the song, which were feeling more and more suffocated inside her, decide to come out, when she is sleeping. The song becomes a man's coat and the story becomes a man's pair of shoes. They hang outside the house. The husband comes home and finds someone's coat and shoes. 'What's happening? Who is visiting'? he asks. The woman doesn't know anything about it. 'What are you talking about'? she says. Word follows word, and they get very angry. They quarrel. The man says, 'I'm not going to stay here'. And he goes to the local Hanuman temple, the monkey god's temple, which is usually a little outside the village. He goes there to sleep. He takes his blanket and goes off.

The usual belief is that when a light is put out the flame is not simply extinguished. The flame goes to the monkey god's temple. So all the flames of the lamps put out in the village would come to the monkey god's temple and be there until the next day when the people would light their lamps again. These flames know every secret in the family. And they gossip. They talk about what's happening with their families.

On this particular day, one comes late—the flame from the man's house. The woman has not put out the light because she's worried. 'What is happening to me? Why is this man so angry? I've done nothing'. Finally she puts out the lamp and goes to sleep, so her flame comes late to the temple.

All the other flames ask, 'What's happening? Why are you late? You used to be early'. And the flame says, 'There was a big quarrel in the house'. And it explains what happened to the other flames. 'The lady of the house knew a story and a song, but she never told them. Today they took revenge. They came out and became a man's coat and a pair of shoes. The husband became very angry. She doesn't even know it.'

The husband hears all this. He goes home. By this time it's early morning. He asks the woman, 'It seems you know a story and a song'. She says, 'What story? What song?' You see, she doesn't even know she had them. She's lost them.

That's a story about telling stories and not telling stories. And why they should be told.

ALB: Would you call that a breakfast, lunch, or dinner story?

AKR: More night. Definitely a dinner story.

KT: We see now, coming into the literatures of what were the colonial languages, stories from what were the colonized societies. Probably the example everybody would know these days would be Salman Rushdie.

AKR: And this new book, *The Empire Writes Back*. People should know that.

KT: We see that this new impulse is going to change our traditional understanding of our literatures ...

AKR: And also the understanding of our traditional texts. So far Indians or Chinese or Africans have not truly interpreted Shakespeare, for instance. They have simply gone to England, learned methods of criticism there, and gone home. If you read an Indian writing about Shakespeare or English literature, it would not be seriously different from what you already know.

KT: What do you mean by a true interpretation?

AKR: Not true. Did I say true? No. What I meant was ... the way, for instance, Jan Kott, coming from an Eastern European country, writes in *Shakespeare, Our Contemporary*, and sees in *Hamlet* or *The Tempest* a political vision.

For instance, *The Tempest* has been used by a number of people now to speak of colonialism. And it's a very clear picture of colonialism.

KT: The treatment of Caliban, even the figure of Caliban.

ALB: And Ariel.

AKR: And the island itself. Prospero having control over everything. He needs Caliban to show him where the berries are, where the water is. He teaches him the language. An Englishman teaches Caliban English. The profit of it is, that the colonized then know how to curse you. That's what Shakespeare is saying. That's what Caliban says.

So there's plenty, including the language and the introduction of whiskey, the underlings that become the great gods of the natives—point by point there are so many parallels between an imposition of a colonial regime on these countries which were seen as almost virgin countries. In Shakespeare's play they're seen as virgin countries. In fact, a country like India is certainly not that kind of virgin country. We already had a long civilization. But that's not what the colonizers thought.

Macaulay's Minute in 1835 says 'All the texts of Sanskrit could be bartered for one play of Shakespeare'. And he thought Indian medicine was mumbo-jumbo. And the cosmology was, what does he call it? 'Seas of treacle.'

ALB: Sounds like Saul Bellow's great-grandfather.

AKR: Well, he was quite contemptuous of our entire civilization. He thought of the coming of English into these languages and cultures as a kind of civilizing force. It was the 'white man's burden'.

In reverse, of course, now there is the brown man's burden. All these Indians who come to this country and feel they should spiritualize and civilize the materialist man.

ALB: Revenge.

KT: Would the creation of postcolonial literatures be a variation of that?

AKR: No. There's the purely reactive aspect of it. That is, we leave countries that have been oppressed, that have been colonized not merely physically but also intellectually. There is no critical idiom in these countries that has not been brought in from the West. I was once making a list of all the words we use in describing Indian things and saw how many of the words have no native roots. Even words like literature, history, words like society, nation, state. None of these—probably even the word caste—has a clear-cut Indian language translation. All of these have come to us through the interaction of native thinking and Englishmen imposing ideas on us.

ALB: It's interesting that all the South East Asian languages have that relationship to Indian culture. Sanskrit is the metalanguage and all the words have come from that. So it's a transitive kind of thing.

AKR: Yes, of course it is. But it doesn't mean that Indians have forgotten Sanskrit or anything like that. It's not privileged. The number of people who study Sanskrit today is small. How many people know Sanskrit? If you take the number of Indians who know Sanskrit and the number who know English, the former is much smaller.

KT: Even though the religious texts are in Sanskrit ...

AKR: And there are people who know the texts well. There are two things that will happen in the postcolonial world. One is the studying and translation of the great texts of these literatures. And not just new literatures. Tamil, for instance, has a literary tradition almost two thousand years old. And a language like Kannada has one that goes back a thousand years. It's longer than what you will find in English. The discovery of these things by people outside the country, people outside even the language ... you must not forget that Bengalis don't know Kannada. And the Kannada speakers don't know Punjabi ... so internally, too, Indians have to discover one another's languages and cultures. That is just beginning to happen. There are many more poetry festivals, for instance, where Punjabi poets and Hindi poets and Bengali poets come together and read one another's translations. These things happen mainly through English, by the way. So a lot is going to happen.

Just as we Indians don't know Indonesian. It's not enough to say people are Asians. We don't know one another. How many Indians know Chinese? How many Chinese know any of the Indian languages? A handful, if that.

ALB: It's one thing to know Sanskrit, it's another to be living in it, so that your everyday vocabulary has its fragrance. There's something you might call believing in Sanskrit.

AKR: For most of us, that is simply not there. But you must remember that if I speak in Kannada, there will be a lot of Sanskrit in my language. So Sanskrit, like English, is reflected in our languages. I sometimes think that the greatest effect of English is how it is reflected in our languages. All our modern poets will know English. They would have been influenced by Eliot and Yeats and so on. They would have written new kinds of poems. Sanskrit, too, has done that to our languages. The *Rāmāyaṇa* is retold in all our languages. It is completely different from what it is in Sanskrit. It is still positioned in Sanskrit. In that sense, the Sanskrit is not dead.

ALB: But I want to stick on this point. In the special status of Sanskrit, in Sanskrit as the original language, is that still believed by a speaker of Kannada or Hindi?

AKR: Not always. There's still a small number of people who believe in it. There are, of course, the revivalists. Hindu revivalists. On the other hand, you still find Sanskrit used in temples, in worship. Sanskrit is still used in all weddings. There is a kind of magical quality, a ritual quality to Sanskrit. It is not simply thrown away. But it's not everywhere. That's one thing.

And the second thing is—one of the great realizations I've had to come to—that Sanskrit is not the only religious language. By the fifth century, religious poetry is written in the mother tongues. Tamil is one of the first of these. And that becomes part of the temple services. Like the poems I've translated from the medieval *vacanas*, for instance. Every Vīraśaiva temple in south India, for instance, will sing those poems. So even within India, people who may have known no Sanskrit still had a religious language.

So, like I said, one of my agendas has been to see from that side where Sanskrit was not enough. It was important, but it was not everything. It gives you only one view of India. Certainly what was exported to Indonesia was Sanskrit.

ALB: It seems to me that India was always exported as a tremendous diversity. All of these religions, all of these gods, all of these possibilities, all of these languages ... into Burma, Malaysia, all of South East Asia.

AKR: You're right about that. Thailand has Tamil poems and Tamil rituals. Some of the poems found there are from the seventh century.

ALB: But Sanskrit in the rest of South East Asia has a status different from other languages. For a translator, for a poet, for anybody else, this special status is extremely important. The Sanskrit words, the Sanskrit roots, the Sanskrit metaphors, seem nearer to source, nearer to originality.

KT: That's still an active belief in other countries of South East Asia?

ALB: From Bali down.

AKR: I am probably the wrong person to talk about this. I suppose I'm ideologically radical towards Sanskrit.

ALB: That's interesting. How did that come about?

AKR: Like I said, partly my reaction to the Hindu caste system and my associations with Brahmanism. I came from a Brahman family, so I could have it both ways. That is, I could have all the privileges of being a Brahman and also have all the privileges of reacting against it. My discovery over the years is that the mother tongues have so much in them, so much that is alive, and are much more pervasive, in all strata of society, in all ages from children to the very old, men and women, literate and non-literate. What holds them together? It's not Sanskrit. It's these mother tongues. I think I went into linguistics because of that. These spoken tongues had to be very, very important. It was important to me in my youth to have discovered this.

ALB: It runs counter in some ways to the current trends toward universalism, to the idea that we ought to have fewer languages. Your position would be that the diversity of the mother tongues would be central to ...

AKR: Not only that. Without that diversity language would not express intimately the reality of the life of these people as it is lived. These people are not one. There are hundreds of different kinds of people and each must have a language of their own, which is what they have in India. And then there is my interest in dialect. The 1971 census gives us three thousand names for mother tongues in India. They have asked people, 'What do you speak'? And they have been given three thousand names. Now these don't mean three thousand languages. These are three thousand speech varieties, which people consider special to themselves. Linguists come along later and classify them and say there are about 100 or 105 languages in India. And four different language families.

But what I think we call folklore, even what we call self-expression, is found in these three thousand dialects. Nobody will accept that. They will say, any single language that we call Kannada or so on already suppresses a great deal of diversity.

ALB: You're saying that you want that diversity.

AKR: I want the diversity!

KT: Wouldn't some Indian politicians ask for a universal language in India?

AKR: Unity. Of course, they've wanted it for a long time. There's been pressure for Hindi to be the language, because it is spoken by a plurality of people, over 130 or 140 million.

KT: Whereas Kannada is spoken by twenty million ...

AKR: More than that. And Tamil is spoken by fifty million. Bengali is spoken by over eighty million. These are not small numbers!

KT: No. These are very large numbers. Much larger than the number of people speaking modern Greek.

AKR: Greek. Or Finnish. Or Israeli Hebrew. Each of the Indian regional languages covers a lot of diversity. Say if you take a place like the Kannada-speaking region in south India, there are a dozen languages which are being spoken there by minorities. In any big city in India, there will be a dozen languages being spoken, with one dominant language. One has to be sensitive to all the languages. Of course, this is politically very difficult. India needs a different kind of system where language difference is not an area of conflict. But that's not what has happened.

ALB: There are two things which run through your work in an interesting way. One of them has to do with the richness of the mother tongues. The power that comes from the multiplicity of languages. The other comes through the area where I knew you first as a writer— the translations from Tamil poetry. It is interesting to see the degree to which that poetry was produced by a small community that sustained itself with a kind of purity for many hundreds of years. That Caṅkam (pronounced Sangam) community ...

AKR: It lasted 250 years, probably. And it was probably non-Sanskritic.

ALB: But there are two things. There's the power we have recognized that comes from cultural diversity. Then there's the power that comes through the translations that seems to come from a kind of cultural purity. A lot of shared vocabulary ...

AKR: Purity is not a word I want to use. Simply because I've never found it anywhere.

ALB: But there's the myth of the Caṅkam. You say in one of your introductions that it was almost as if this poetry, written over hundreds of years, was written by one person.

AKR: Or by a group of interacting people.

ALB: But that only could be possible with a kind of uniformity that was sustained over a long period.

AKR: And it was a very small community. These chiefdoms—they were not even kingdoms in the beginning—these chiefdoms were not more than 200 square miles. Very small.

ALB: But still, this is a powerful poetry. It wasn't an accident that, for many of us in this country, your voice as a creative person came through the Tamil translations in *The Interior Landscape* first. And part of the power comes from discovering this unified society behind the poetry. The excitement comes from recognizing that. Over this whole period and through this whole canon, we have certain roles recurring. Certain roles, certain places.

AKR: Right.

ALB: Certain moods, which are established, set.

AKR: I don't know if it was so in the society outside of it, but it was so in the Caṅkam.

ALB: I'm interested in the public/private theme that comes up in Ramanujan's poetry. In a way, there are two poetries: the interior and the exterior. That seems to resonate with the older Tamil poems. For me, as an outsider, I have a hard time distinguishing between the two. When I read the translations of Tamil poetry, my first take is that this is Ramanujan's poetic power taking something and giving it life. The next week I go back and read it and say—this is a tremendous society. This is an unusual society. The Caṅkam, mythological and possibly elitist as it was, was the kind of community of scholars that all of us dream about: scholars and poets and artists who are living together and building a tradition. I never know whether to attribute this to your creation or to the original texts.

AKR: I don't know either. When I first published these poems in *The Interior Landscape,* there were Indian friends of mine, and people who knew Indian poetry well, who knew the whole tradition of Sanskrit ... they all said to me, 'This cannot be Indian poetry'. It looked so different from anything they had ever seen. It was not flamboyant. It didn't have all those hyperbolic and formulaic restrictions on women, and so on. It's only when I showed them the originals and translated them almost word for word, that they began to see that these things were all there—mediated of course by what I could do with it, or what I could see of it. Part of the excitement of that work was my own discovery of these texts.

KT: You give a description of coming across the texts in a library ...

AKR: Yes. You see I came to Chicago as a linguist, to teach Tamil.

Then I thought, how can I do this? I need to know classical Tamil. I didn't know classical Tamil. I wasn't educated in the Tamil-speaking areas of India, so I never knew the classical language. I came to it completely innocently. I think that ignorance was a great asset. I was not taught by pundits. Now I've lost a lot by not being taught by pundits. I would have learned a lot from them. I learned from them afterwards. But I came to it simply because I wanted to study the poetry. I was not interested in the tradition, I was interested in single poems, as I always am. That made me see things in the poetry which I had not seen before. Anywhere. Because my translations came without the knowledge of the tradition, I think there was a kind of freshness or innocence which allowed me to see things there that other people had not seen before.

The two kinds of satisfactions—both of them rare—that have come to me with those translations are: first, when complete foreigners who know nothing about India are able to read them, and the poems are used in weddings and things like that; the other satisfaction is when a native Indian who knew the poetry from childhood reads it and says, 'I have not seen that poem like that before'. It doesn't happen every day. When it does, it's very gratifying. Then I feel a translation was worth having done.

ALB: You have written that your goal is not just to translate the poems but to translate the reader. Part of the success of that book and of the later *Poems of Love and War* was the degree to which you've succeeded in translating the reader. You did that in part through fine translations and awfully fine poetry.

AKR: It's the poetry that really conveys itself.

ALB: But the afterword is a large part of the book. In a way it's not an afterword—it's essential for understanding that poetry.

AKR: Surely. In *The Interior Landscape*, I discovered that I couldn't leave the translations just like that. So I say that there are three parts to these books. One is the poems themselves. The second is the notes. And the third is the afterword. The translation consists of all three of them. It is true that the notes and the afterword are confessions of failure for a translator. If I were a perfect translator, I wouldn't need them. I'm not. But I feel that all three of them together translate the poems.

ALB: How seriously do we want to take you right now when you say that if you were a perfect translator we wouldn't need the notes? I can't imagine a world where, given the differences between languages, that could be possible.

AKR: You may be right. I used to feel that every note I write to a poem is a confession of a failure. But I knew I could never do without it. There are any number of things that, if I really put them into the poem, would not make a good translation, would clutter the poem. I couldn't put in that sort of factual information.

ALB: I think one of the problems with discussions about translation is just that. People always think that if the translators were just better, there would be no need for notes or afterwords. But if we really do think of translating the reader as part of it, the notes and afterwords become co-equal with the poems. Isn't there a different aesthetic if we accept translating the reader as a goal?

AKR: Also the acceptance that all translations are compromises. It is the art of the imperfect. Literatures are so deeply grounded in their cultures and in the cultures they carry ... To cross from one language to another—which is, after all, what translation means—is a very imperfect business. And there is much damage in translating. But there it has to be pointed to, and in the pointing itself some of the damage is undone. In showing what can be done, the reader can make the leaps that are necessary.

ALB: In this sense it's not just a problem with translation. It is a problem in everyday conversation, or with something like this interview, the thing we're doing right now. The word imperfection suggests that there is a perfect conversation, a perfect interview.

AKR: Sometimes there is a kind of dream that there is a seamless communication. Two people sit together and there is perfect understanding. Like in the old Indian poem—the guru was silent; the disciple was silent; and still everything was said. And that is, of course, a dream. Once you open your mouth, that dream is ruptured.

ALB: What I'm driving at is that there is a sense in which your two worlds—Indian and English-speaking—are one, in dealing with this kind of imperfection.

AKR: There is some new work that is being written about my poetry, and they are beginning to discover that there is so much allusion in my poems, my English poems, which I have never talked about.

KT: Allusion to Indian ...

AKR: Indian materials. All kind of materials. Both Indian and western. I write with what I know.

KT: Yes. There's a fair amount of literary reference. I ran across the line in your poem, 'Conventions of Despair': ' "eye-deep" in those Boiling Crates of Oil'.

AKR: Which is Pound.

KT: From 'Hugh Selwyn Mauberley', right? Doesn't that go back to Dante, too?

AKR: I actually put it in quotes. Very few people have noticed those quotes. But that's part of my expressive means. I've read Pound, and I've read Indian things. I think with them. Why shouldn't I use what I have?

ALB: You said recently at a reading that you try very hard to keep your own poetry and your translation separate. That you felt awkward putting the two on the same programme.

AKR: You know I am overwhelmed by these poems that I translate. I think they are some of the great poems of all time. I hesitate to put my own poems next to them. I feel that the tones are different. The translations require some kind of explication which my poems don't want.

ALB: Here again, though, there seems to be a kind of public poem and a private poem, a mother poem and an outside-the-house poem. You strive to keep them separate.

AKR: Oh, no. Separate only in the readings. There is a lot of interpenetration between them. I'm also a little afraid that people may compare my poems to the others. I don't like the competition.

ALB: For most of the world, those other poems are only to be heard in your voice.

AKR: That's true. I must not underestimate the fact that in translating them I have to use my own voice. I am not the kind of translator who is a ventriloquist, who can become the voice of the ancient poet. I also don't believe in that. Ultimately the language you translate into comes from yourself. As hard as you try, you just cannot get away from it. It has to come from your expressive needs.

ALB: Suppose on this issue, of the individual voice, you were sitting down with one of the ancient Tamil poets, one of the Cankam. Do you think that they would understand the problem?

AKR: But they had no translation. These poets had written for a community that was almost monolingual. They were not thinking of translators. They were not thinking that two thousand years from now somebody would translate these poems, then somebody in England or Australia or Ann Arbor would read them. They wrote for their little Tamil corner. I was very moved when I discovered that I somehow became the little link between them—who didn't care one bit or were unaware of what Shakespeare called 'of accents unborn, accents unknown'. Here I was doing them for myself and they were opening out for all kinds of people. That is not what they were written for. They were done for that little court, that little chiefdom.

ALB: The skill and the beauty were not motivated by the idea, 'Let me find my original voice'. It was more, 'Let me write a poem that is worthy of this canon'. It would be much more like writing another act for *King Lear* than it would be writing a new poem. They were trying to become a part of this big poem that was almost one voice.

AKR: That Harold Bloom notion of 'anxiety of influence' just doesn't apply to this. They want the influence. They have all apprenticed themselves to the master. This is the way traditional Indian musicians will learn. They will sit behind the singer and sing along with him, just droning. Then, gradually, the master will ask the disciple to join his voice to his. He will do it for several years. At the end of it the master is gone, and the disciple is left to sing the song. It is through imitation that you learn. It is through following in the master's line. This was true of the poets and every other artist. The notion of the Prague school and others, the notion where poetics is a violation of language, is also not true here. There is no defamiliarity of language. The defamiliarization takes place in the freshness of vision. There is no violation of language; it is the fulfilment of tradition. The poet says, 'I will show one more thing that the tradition can do'.

ALB: The man that you quote in your talks about this poetry seems to me a remarkable man. The Aristotle. Tolkāppiyar.

AKR: Yes. The man who wrote the poetics. He was also a grammarian. He does it all for Tamil! Rhetoric, prosody, and poetics. He's very close to what you would call a linguist's ultimate guru. He does everything. He takes all of language, from the most ordinary banal language to the most poetic, as the subject of his linguistics.

ALB: He seems to be someone whose bust we should be putting in our libraries.

KT: OK. Let's back up and get Pete to define what he thinks linguistics ought to be doing, why he thinks Tolkāppiyar was so extraordinary.

ALB: No! We're not interviewing me.

AKR: But you and I agree on that. So go ahead.

ALB: For me, the most important and interesting question about the study of language is, 'What does it take for me as a speaker of English, what kinds of changes in me are necessary, to be able to understand a Tamil poem from the inside?' It's what my teacher, Ken Pike, used to call emicity. Anything that is a part of that process of moving from within one culture to another culture—and I tend to think of language and culture as identical—is what linguistics is about. It's about the medium; it's about memory; the writing system itself. Looking at Tamil poetry, for instance, I would be fascinated to know what changed in the translation from the Tamil script into the Roman letters. How the world changes when you change writing systems.

AKR: I would distinguish between language and culture, though you couldn't get one without the other. Language as a system is somewhat separable. But if you separate them entirely, you get an impoverished linguistics. You need the culture to fully enter that language.

Linguistics ought to be the study of language in all its forms. By and large, linguistics has been the study of the banal. Linguists have trouble with questions like what could be metaphor or what is a figure of speech. They can't write a formula for it, or they can't do a transformation. When they do, it is so cumbersome; the machinery is so large. This reminds me of that cartoon in *Punch*. There is a room full of machinery, with cogs and wheels. A man comes in and presses the button. Everything moves, grinds, and finally there is a little light for his cigarette. Sometimes linguistics seems to be that sort of thing. There has been a great deal of achievement in formal linguistics in recent years.

KT: Now, go back and fill me in. The Tamil grammarian, Tolkāppiyar, his bust should go up in our libraries, because ...

ALB: Because he opened up that Tamil world with a kind of care and thoughtfulness and imagination that is certainly comparable to Plato or Aristotle in the western world. The way that he took the least part of things we do with language and subjected it to careful analysis ... not so much to make the rules as to describe it. When was he working? Was he after the Caṅkam?

AKR: Probably. Or somewhere in the middle of the Caṅkam. By the time the Caṅkam is over, so is Tolkāppiyar.

ALB: But he describes it with care and distinction. He says there are different ways of doing this, and here's what they are. Did it become prescriptive?

AKR: Later. Not very long after. By the time we come to the fifth century, the whole tradition changes. You get religious poems. They begin to use the Caṅkam poems as a kind of base for writing religious poems. Already in the fourth or fifth century you begin to get parodies of the Caṅkam poems. In the latter part of *Poems of Love and War*, I give all those poems, which are really comic poems. The society is already changing. It is no longer the society of the elite. There is a lot of folk poetry which is making fun of the tradition.

ALB: One of the quotations I always enjoy from Clifford Geertz is that 'art and the equipment to grasp it are made in the same shop'. Tolkāppiyar is important because here we have someone describing the equipment to grasp art, describing the conventions, describing in such detail everything that is taken for granted by the people. So what we get in your books is more than the Tamil poetry. We get the equipment to grasp it. That's what translating the reader is all about, isn't it?

AKR: Which is where you need the afterword and the notes. An educated Tamil reader would be aware of all this. If you want to bring a foreign reader anywhere close to the Tamil reader, he should also have the background. But the poems should educate the reader. I almost never publish these poems in small groups, but try to do whole books of them. These poems build a world and the world they build interprets the poems. It's a circle. One has to do a kind of metonymy, a representation of a whole. There are two thousand poems. I translate only two hundred. But these two hundred are chosen in such a way that they are a true sample. I try to do a smaller replica of the structured world of the poems. But you don't get that with a single poem. A single poem does not exist by itself. It exists only in the ambiance of all the other poems.

KT: Although a poem like the one you quote right at the beginning of your introduction to *Speaking of Śiva* would be a fairly easy poem to take out and put in an anthology.

AKR: But then, as you can see, I write three pages on that poem.

KT: Which helps.

ALB: Which explains a lot of things.

AKR: A sophisticated native reader would be explicitly aware of the terminology.

ALB: With such riches as this large body of untranslated poetry to work with, what made you turn recently to folktales?

AKR: For one thing, they are very exciting stories. Folktales are addressed to the childhood world and come out of the childhood world. The poems are from a more adult world. Of course, no adult is cut off from the folktales. He is constantly resonating to those tales whether he is 5 years old or 50. Secondly, the folktale world is a counterpoint to the big official world—the world of the epics, of the mythologies, which you constantly hear about and which are translated everywhere. The folktales are a countersystem to the ideology of the epics.

ALB: So it's like the movement from father to mother tongue. It's a movement from father to mother story.

AKR: Well, yes. But even within the mother tongue, there are standard texts. These folktales are not written texts. They are supposed to be ephemeral. Except these texts have also lived a very long time. They have lived long not because someone has written them down but because they are constantly being told. And constantly changing.

I'm very interested in various kinds of psychologies. These folktales have a native psychology. Unlike the mythologies, the tales have to do with families, with father and son, father and daughter, mother and daughter. So many times there are rules broken in folktales. For instance, incest is very common in folktales. So this focus in the folktales on the family, on the relationships—not merely man/woman relationships—is essential.

ALB: It seems very complementary to the poetry that you translate.

AKR: Yes. In the classical Tamil texts, the household world and the outside world are distinguished. War is a part of the outside world. The language of the household poetry is the language of love, the language of intimate relationships. All the problems between a man and a woman are part of this, the interior poetry.

In terms of genres, the folktales live out of the interior language. Mythologies are part of the outer world. They have to do with wars. All the gods have a great many wars. They construct cosmologies and deal with social issues. In the folktales, everything is interiorized. You don't see the big social issues except through the detail of intimate relationships.

ALB: Did you ever try to write a folktale?

AKR: I have written folktales, basically imitating the ones I know. They are usually comic. But I wasn't satisfied. The real ones are so good, in the sense that they have been polished by the tellers over a long period—over the centuries! No single person could do something like that. Every detail is in place. A good teller would know how to displace something and put in another detail.

It's been said that 'a tradition is a sentence polished by generations'. In the folktales the sentences are not polished—everything is kept quite simple on that level. But the focus on the narrative, on these intimate relationships, is perfect, even though the character is completely flat. The total plot is what carries the subtlety. The tales are psychological not in the sense that modern novels are psychological. Folktales never show the interior monologues of a character. But the total picture conveys a psychology, like the story I told you earlier. It takes the man a journey outside his house, to the temple where he hears the gossip of the flames, before he understands what is happening inside his own house. The subtlety of that is extraordinary.

ALB: There is one issue I want to make sure we touch on. It has to do with these two traditions and the present. The folktale tradition builds over time. The love poetry from the classical Tamil gives a picture of continuity over time. Now, your colleagues at Chicago, some of the Committee on Social Thought, are associated with one side of this: the notion of the canon of literature. For many of us in this country, they seem to have a right-wing attitude. An attitude which is trying to foist an elitism on a democratic, changing country. It's racist, it's sexist, and all that. They are protecting the literatures of European males. But there is a power in the folktales, that at their best people like Saul Bellow and Allan Bloom are trying to find. Maybe we think they're getting at it the wrong way. Now, you are someone from another culture who knows these attitudes very well. I would be interested in some of your thoughts on this American controversy.

AKR: There are two things to be said about this. These people are quite sophisticated. They are not simply prejudiced. If they have prejudices, they are prejudices with which they have reasoned. They are not simply prejudices which they have inherited. First, somebody like Bellow is open to a lot of things, whatever may be his public presentation of them. He certainly would be open to literature wherever he finds it.

You see, we're back to the earlier problems. There are not enough translations of the other language.

For something like Homer, you have good translations and bad translations. Every generation makes its own translation of Homer. But who is making those for Indian literature? Or African literature? Or Chinese literature? There is no self-correcting tradition of translation from these languages. That leaves no way in which readers can truly enter these works. If you want to enlarge the canon, it's not enough to say I will include an African text or an Indian text. If you include bad translations, translations which are wrong, you would be doing a disservice to these literatures. You would be comparing the best work of the West, of which you are a native, with a very bad representation of even the best work of my culture.

So, of course, it is good to talk about enlarging the canon of literature. But we have to do it in such a way that people have access to the best. It is essential that we have become sensitive to this issue. But we do not want to get a token text. Most people would respond to it negatively.

It's good to open the canon, or whatever you want to call it. I just got a letter from people at Cornell who are trying to do an encyclopedia of global literacy. They want to include non-western texts. We need that sort of thing. But it's not enough to simply have information. If you want to read Plato, for instance, you can read it in the best translations. And the translations have been criticized for generations; you have corrections and commentary. Where is that happening for other texts? We can't simply say we're going to make a list of these other works and add them to our reading lists. We would be doing an unequal reading.

KT: But wouldn't building up a tradition in the West of this kind of close reading of other work take hundreds of years?

AKR: No. We are already coming up with new translators. But many of the academic departments at our universities, like Asian or South East Asian departments, have to prepare translators—not just make translations by committee. We need translators. It's not enough to have the golden egg; we must have the goose.

ALB: Then we must find a way to support translators. Very few translators have been able to sustain themselves by their work.

AKR: Good translators are so rare. And then with a good translation, the work must choose the translator and the translator the work. It's not simply the NEH making a list and looking for people to do it. If so and so knows Javanese, have him do it. No. It needs to be more than that. We need centres where we're constantly looking for translators.

ALB: We could say that a new genre is opening up. And we could call it translating the reader. That would be a very different art to learn.

AKR: For this we need to have translation workshops. Just like we have poetry or fiction workshops. Places where people share the languages they know. No wildly different languages. If the five or six people who know Javanese well enough in America could get together and do a translation workshop, then a great deal could be done. This is not a workshop where you translate from French, I translate from German, and someone else translates from Javanese. That implies that there is a universality to all the problems. That's not true. If four people who know Javanese get together and read one another's work, then much more relevant critiques are possible.

Then you would get enough talk about things. For example, the Committee on Social Thought, where Allan Bloom teaches, has two of us who are Indianists. Then there is a Chinese translator, Tony Yu. And there are students there who will take Indian classics as well as the western ones. These are new roads.

KT: Yet there does seem to be an attitude in Bloom's popular book, *The Closing of the American Mind,* that seems to be trying to build a stockade around western culture.

AKR: That's not a true representation. The only thing that I would disagree with Bloom about, which is a central thing, is the notion that the liberal traditions of the world can be found only in the West. Bloom is not alone in this attitude. You find it in the work of Naipaul. You find it in earlier people, like Hegel, and others who have written on democracies: the notion that traditional cultures like the Chinese, or the Indian, or the African, are not capable of thinking through a rational, liberal, democratic way of politics or philosophy. That notion is at the back of their thinking. Someone like Bloom will say when you talk about anthropology, 'Where before the West was there any curiosity about other cultures'? Now, he has his troubles with anthropology. As a humanist, he thinks the social sciences are not humane enough. But he has this idea of 'only in the West ...'. He'll say Herodotus was the first person who looked at the Persians or the Indians. You will not find an Indian historian or thinker writing about the West that way.

Or Bloom will say that the kind of rational inquiry you find in Plato, you cannot find outside the West. Of course, he's wrong. He just doesn't know enough about India or China.

ALB: Is that ignorance or is that a challenge?

AKR: It is partly ignorance. Partly he doesn't know the texts, but partly he believes that. There is a claim Bloom makes. That claim has to be taken seriously, by other scholars—say departments of African studies or Indian studies. We have to examine these ideas, not simply dismiss them as racist. They should be taken as a serious challenge and talked about. That would make for fruitful dialogue.

KT: Could Allan Bloom be convinced?

AKR: Whether he's convinced or not is another matter. The question is out there on the table, so it should be discussed by people. Then Bloom has done a valuable service.

ALB: So tell me, to quote an article of yours, is there an Indian way of thinking?

AKR: I don't know. Let's leave it as a question. There is no categorical answer. If you say 'yes', then someone will immediately ask, 'What is it?' I would say that there is a particular configuration, the components of which probably are everywhere. Or elsewhere. I would not say that the logic of the Indian is different from anyone else's. But the context of thought, the function of thought in society—in all of that there would be certain slants, certain biases.

ALB: Is it possible to say there is a Tamil way of thinking?

AKR: Once you ask the first question, then you get this. And the Tamils would say, 'Of course there is. And it's better'. Although it makes more sense to bring the question down to a language rather than a subcontinent. There is so much variety within a language, to say there is a single pattern is impossible. Let's say there is a certain bias within the thought systems of one language which seems to be similar over time. It is what I was saying about contextivity. Nothing makes sense out of context.

KT: You write poems in both Kannada and English. Is there a different context in your mind when you are working in one or the other language?

AKR: No. It is, after all, the same person writing the poems. But the different languages bring with them different constraints, different points of reference. The Kannada culture now includes a lot of English. In the three languages I know well, whichever one I am working in, the other two are present. I am not a *tabula rasa*. I always think about my languages as certain kinds of musical instruments. If you pluck one string there are other strings which resonate. Like the Indian sitar, there are strings which the musician never touches. They are resonating strings. It is like that for all of us. Everything we know is resonating with what we talk about in the foreground.

Of course, if I am writing a poem in Kannada, I am aware of the tradition and the contemporary practice. There's a kind of elegance that is *de rigueur* in Kannada poetry, what I would call writing at the top of the voice. It's very declamatory. Someone like me comes along and may not want to write that way. I may write the opposite kind of poetry, much more colloquial, more low key, talking about ordinary things. Influenced by people like William Carlos Williams, I carve out of ordinary language and ordinary experience a shape. When I'm writing English poetry, I may do the opposite of what other poets are doing.

KT: I've noticed that. Some of your recent poetry has been in traditional English forms.

AKR: Yes. If everybody's writing free verse, I'll see if I can get away with something else.

KT: In some of your recent things in English, I would think of Auden as more of an influence than Williams.

AKR: Yes. I want to do that to expand my own way of writing. I could be doing two opposite things in the different languages.

ALB: You give an example of a wonderful multicultural world. It's utopian in a way. The kind of sensitivity you're asking for is difficult.

AKR: Well, it's not necessary to know all the languages. It's not possible. Within each life, if we could know two or three languages, if we could fully cultivate them, and cultivate our mother tongues more deeply, then we would be moving in a positive direction.

ALB: But the forces of universalism seem to be so overwhelming right now. Some days I don't have hope for the kind of diversity you're holding up as an ideal.

AKR: Just as in economics there is an internationalization of the market, there is also an internationalization of culture. A modern poet writing a modernist poem in Kannada is very much like one writing a poem in Africa or England or China. I was just at the poetry festival in Jerusalem. I was struck by the commonality of the influence.

ALB: It is a more powerful force than the diversity of mother tongues.

AKR: We have to struggle to find our local voices.

ALB: These local traditions may be wiped out by the commonality.

AKR: Cosmopolitanism has always been there. It's stronger now because of all the travel. Look at the clothes. Jeans. Pop music. English of a certain sort. Wherever you go, you will see the same things.

KT: What was that recent book, *Video Nights in Kathmandu?*

AKR: Exactly. For a lot of people the local will be wiped out. Those people were probably dependent for all entertainment on the local. Now they have the juke box or TV.

ALB: It's a rough time for language cultures. Some of them aren't going to make it.

AKR: Oh, no. It doesn't mean people won't be writing in their languages. Not everybody is going to write in English. Most people can't. They have to write in a language that is continuous with their childhood.

ALB: But a lot of the North American Indian languages, for instance, are in this generation going to die.

AKR: Yes. Part of the problem is the smallness of the population. And they are powerless. They don't have states of their own. That is not happening in India and Africa. There's a lot of powerful regionalism there. But, still, certain tribal languages will suffer the same fate. You must have a population and you must have political power for a language to survive. The Native Americans are fighting for it. Meanwhile it seems as if they are losing, culturally. They are becoming businessmen and office workers.

ALB: The reaction in Malaysia to my translation of the *Hikayat Hang Tuah*, the Malaysian epic, was: 'That's too bad. Now no one will read it in Malay'. To them, there's a sense of threat in translation.

AKR: Some of the threat is real. But that will never be true in a country like India. Many of the people who would read a Kannada epic in the original would never read it comfortably in English.

ALB: But there is a struggle here. We have a hard time selling multiculturalism to a lot of the forces in the world.

AKR: There is a struggle. But the one-language forces have never succeeded. It might be good that English is so widespread as a second language. English has distorted our traditions, but it has also made us look at our traditions. It's not enough to say that it is all colonialism and has done nothing but distort. This whole question of colonial distortion has been formulated in English. It requires a dialogue with English. English has been the 'other' through which we have returned to ourselves. English has become a part of us. To say we want to return to a pre-English state is chimerical. The anti-colonial discourse is all done in English. Nobody's writing this in Kannada. In India, there is a wonderful group of new historians called the Subalterns, who are looking at all the distortions of the colonial intellectual practices. But all their work is done in English. Isn't the English in which they are writing distorting what they are writing about? English has made us self-critical and made us critical of English itself.

ALB: And it has helped English.

KT: We still might be just at the beginning of the influence on us, on English.

ALB: Look back at American English, American literature, back to Emerson, and look at the influence of Indian literature. There has long been that bridge from Indian literature to English.

AKR: Those ships that carried ice from Boston to Calcutta. Walden Pond and Ganges.

KT: With all your different hats—poet, translator, linguist, folklorist, anthropologist—is there a hat you would choose?

AKR: No. I don't know if I wear all those hats. I seem to be doing the same thing in all the disciplines. The notion that there is a line to be drawn between different interests is not true. Everything we have and know is part of the instrument.

UNCOLLECTED PROSE

Like an elephant
lost from his herd
suddenly captured,

remembering his mountains,
    his Vindhyas,
        I remember.

A parrot
come into a cage
remembering his mate,
        I remember.

O lord white as jasmine
show me
your ways.
        Call me: Child, come here,
    come this way.

        Akkamahadevi, woman saint,
        Kannada (twelfth century)
        tr. Ramanujan, 1973, p. 136

THE RING OF MEMORY

Remembering and Forgetting in Indian Literatures*

———◆———

As some lover brought by many prayers
to a lady's side, only to find
that she does not recognize him when he is come
and so all hope of making love to her is gone;
just so is God, although he be
our very soul, misprised within us
and cannot share with us his glory.
Therefore I have written this book called 'Recognition'.

Utpala (q. Ingalls et al., 1990, p. 125)

Here, I shall present a collage of ideas, images, stories, and poems about remembering and forgetting and what they mean to a traditional Hindu; I shall mention in passing some Jaina and Buddhist traditions also. My concern, as in such other papers of mine, is not only to suggest an intellectual pattern but to let my audience, if I can, experience how it feels to hold such ideas, to enter and participate in the Hindu ethos created as it is not just by philosophies but by favourite narratives. I shall end it with a somewhat more detailed analysis of the great Indian play, *Śakuntalā*, by Kālidāsa (fifth century)—which gives this paper its title, 'The Ring of Memory'.

*Perhaps AKR was thinking of writing a book on memory, but all we have is this brilliant fragment among his papers.

The Arts of Memory

Many years ago, I witnessed a remarkable feat of memory. A Jaina monk came to our college, and a performance of his *Aṣṭāvadhāna* was arranged. *Aṣṭāvadhāna* means 'attention to eight things at once'. He was able to do the following eight things simultaneously: he repeated without change a poem that was recited to him by one person, answered several questions in philosophy, arithmetic, or the local newspaper put to him by three others, played a game of dice with another, and a game of chess with still another, completed a half-finished verse recited by a seventh person, and finished by accurately giving us the count of pebbles that were being thrown all the while on his bare back. He could also dictate eight different texts, often compositions of his own, to eight different copyists. I've also heard of *śatāvadhānis* who could simultaneously attend to a hundred such tasks—the simplest of which was to answer in the original order a series of a hundred questions put to him by an audience. These feats displayed skills of both mindfulness and memory. Such arts of memory are part of ancient classical and oral traditions. We know that the Vedas were orally transmitted for centuries before they were written down; even after they were written down they were systematically memorized, gotten by heart, inscribed as it were on the bodies of the reciters. The techniques for acquiring them orally included not only grammatical and phonetic analyses, but various pedagogic methods of marking each uttered phrase physically by various gestures and bodily movements—so that the texts were inscribed almost into the body's motor memory. When I was studying linguistics at Poona, we interviewed an 80-year-old Vedic scholar who could without a moment's pause, repeat any part of the Ṛg Veda from any point to any point, backwards, omitting every other line, give you a concordance of any word or phrase you chose citing its use all through the entire text, and so on. We were the ones who were exhausted at the end of the performance. Indian musicians know all their texts and songs and *rāgas* by heart, Indian epic reciters and orators often use no notes, and I've a friend who once reproduced a poem of mine that I'd lost, which he had seen only once some years earlier. One may of course relate these skills to a learned yet oral tradition. Later, even with literacy and the use of palm-leaf manuscripts, one needed to possess the text orally—as the manuscripts were few, often no more than one, in the possession of a teacher who guarded it like gold. Yet there were other reasons for the cultivation of these arts.

The enlightened sage was said to be a *trikālajñānī*; one who knew time in all its three modes, one who was mindful of the present, knew his entire past (in which this worldview, unlike poorer worldviews, included many past lives), and he saw the future in clear detail as he saw present and past.

Remembering was not a mere skill to show off, it was the means of enlightenment and salvation. The Buddha is said to have complete recall of all his lives. He recounts that prior to his achievement of buddhahood at dawn, he set his mind to the task of recollection:

I directed my mind to the knowledge and recollection of former abodes. I remembered a variety of former abodes: one birth, two births, three births, four births, five births, ten births, twenty births, thirty births, forty births, fifty births, a hundred births, a thousand births, a hundred thousand births, and many aeons of creation, many aeons of destruction, and many aeons of creation and destruction. There I was so named, of such a clan, of such a caste, such food, such experience, of pleasure and pain, such a life span. Passing away there, I appeared elsewhere, and there too I was so named, of such a clan, of such a caste, such food, such experience of pleasure and pain, such a life span. Passing away there, I appeared here. Thus I remembered various former abodes in all their modes and details.

(Lopez, 1992, p. 21)

A certain kind of meditation practice is obviously related to this: one is asked to remember backwards every night, all that one had done or experienced the previous hour, the hour before that and the one before that, and so on, and then to go on to remember the previous day, all the days of the previous month, the previous year, till one could recall the time of one's birth, and then to cross the known to the previous lives. Such practices are related to the exercise of recall, attaining as complete a recollection of one's life as humanly possible— for to remember is to master the past, and thereby get rid of it. In this tradition, 'one remembers in order to forget'. (Compare this with Plato's *anamnesis*, whose end is not to forget but to possess the eternal Forms.) These experts seem to believe literally that he who does not remember the past is condemned to repeat it: Santayana said that about our ignorance of history. Freud thought something similar when he thought that where one cannot or will not remember, one is afflicted with a compulsion to repeat. In Hindu, Jaina or Buddhist conceptions of karma, unacknowledged past actions have a way of imposing their structure on the present, usually with the subject and object reversed, with oneself as the victim and one's former victim as the aggressor in life after life. Thus one's deeds or karma as well as one's memories have a pattern in common: deeds leave behind traces called *saṃskāras,* which persist in future lives, and *vāsanās,* or smells of the past. It is through these that the past structure is revived, whether in memory or in the workings of karma. Only awareness, recollection, re-membering, rising beyond one's 'natural' tendency to forget and erase, only such an act of knowing can release one from the thraldom of repetition and rebirth.

So amnesia is a curse, a form of alienation from one's self, for one's self is largely constituted by memory. Madness or Apasmāra is to misremember, a disorder of memory—the name of the demon Śiva steps on in his cosmic dance is called Apasmāra. The gods themselves fall when they lose their memory (mindfulness, *smara, smṛti*).

In an unpublished study of the wonder tales *(Märchen)* collected in the *Kathāsaritsāgara* ('The Ocean of Story'), Indira Peterson (1980) points out a significant pattern in them. In many of them, a celestial being does something wrong and is cursed to fall, to be reborn as a mortal. 'The focus of the entire tale is on the restoration or return of the protagonist to his former (higher) birth or life; bound with the theme of return are the themes of memory, recognition, knowledge, and recovery of identity.' Let me briefly tell you one of these stories:

A devout king once sees a pair of golden geese flying over his palace. He spends the night longing to see them again. His minister advises him to construct a big lake and arrange for food to be scattered on its banks. When that's done, the golden geese come to the lake and the delighted king spends his days watching them. One day he sees a devotional offering made by the geese and guesses that they could not be mere geese. Anxious to find out who they are, he performs austerities for twelve days. The geese appear to the king in a dream and suggest they meet with him, his queen, and his minister, so that they might tell him the whole truth in private. When they meet, the geese tell the king their past history as follows: 'Because we laughed when we found a pair of attendants engrossed in their love talk when Pārvatī was sad and lovelorn,[1] she cursed us to be reborn as various creatures; the

---

[1]AKR meant to check the original

lovers were cursed to be reborn as mortals, and so was the attendant who tried to intercede. So we were reborn as robbers, dogs, and later crows, vultures, and peacocks, and because of our devotion to Śiva, finally as golden geese'. Then the geese reveal to the king that he and his queen were the lovelorn attendants of Śiva and his consort Pārvatī, and his minister was the attendant who earned a curse by interceding for them. Having attained insight into their past lives and remembering the end of the curse as foretold by Pārvatī, they had now appeared in his dream that night. 'By these means, we have all been reunited today and we will give you the gift of insight'. Then all of them regain their former shapes as celestials and fly back to their heavenly home.

In this much-abridged version, we see how after many lives, they reach the form of golden geese (geese or 'swans' are considered holy birds, emblematic of the soul) when they attain awareness of past lives, remember them as well as the pasts of the king and queen, thereby liberating them all, restoring them to their past lives—achieving, if one wishes to speak in such terms, integration with their own forgotten pasts and their full identities as higher beings. (I am indebted to Peterson's paper for this example and discussion.)

Furthermore, the *Kathāsaritsāgara* is structured as a series of tales told within tales, a character within the first remembering the second tale, and a character within the second remembering the third and so on, and closing each one in a serial order till we return to the frame tale: this characteristic Indian narrative form has multiple functions. In this text, as in other texts like the *Mahābhārata*, which also plays on the logic of karma and the pressures of past lives on the present one, the very form of the multiple-framed story-within-story, each triggering the memory of another relevant story, enacts such an open-ended possibility of multiple lives and recollections, though each tale has an end.

It is not only humans and the lower celestials who forget who they are. The gods themselves forget: Rāma, Kṛṣṇa, and Viṣṇu in the incarnation of Varāha, all forget who they are. At the end of the *Rāmāyaṇa*, Rāma has ruled Ayodhyā for thousands of years and has forgotten that he has to return to his former identity as Viṣṇu. Brahmā comes down and in a secret conference reminds Rāma that he must end his present life on earth and return. In the Kṛṣṇa story, Kṛṣṇa has to fight a deadly black snake in the river; but the poison of the serpent overwhelms him and he loses strength, when his brother Balarāma calls out to him, 'Remember who you are'. When he remembers, all his powers return to him and he conquers the snake and saves the community from its tyranny. There is a charming story told by Rāmakṛṣṇa: in his incarnation as a boar to save the earth-goddess from a demon, Viṣṇu forgets himself. He has a she-boar as a consort and fathers several piglets on her, and he is hogging it, very pleased with himself. When Śiva comes to remind him, he says, 'Leave me alone. I love this pig's life'. Śiva plunges his trident into the boar and releases Viṣṇu from that incarnation.[2]

A Psychology of Memory

According to the doctrine of *vāsanās*—memory traces or smells—perception itself is half memory. One remembers because one sees a partial similarity between the object present and an object one has seen before. So one needs remembrancers so that one may remember, recognize—literally re-member or reconstitute the object in front of us—by reconnecting present impressions with past memories of that object. (Proust too speaks of remembrancers that trigger memories, the taste of the madeleine.)

That brings us to the great Indian play by Kālidāsa, which is a play on memory, lodged in an object that is lost and found, triggering amnesia with its loss and a rush of memories with its retrieval.

Kālidāsa's Abhijñāna Śākuntala

A story is told in the *Mahābhārata* (ll. 62–9) of a king, Duṣyanta, who goes hunting one day, slaughtering many animals, till he comes upon the hermitage of sage Kaṇva and meets Śakuntalā, his foster daughter.

---

[2]An earlier draft of this chapter includes the following paragraph at this point:

Ramakṛṣṇa, the saint and guru, is concerned with this issue of not knowing who one is and tells many parables. In one of them, a pregnant tigress leaps from a high rock and pounces on a flock of sheep. But she falls and dies, giving birth to a tiger cub that the sheep love and take care of, as one of their own. The cub learns to bleat and eat grass and behave like a docile sheep. One day a big tiger comes to the sheepfold. The sheep scatter and run, but the cub, now adolescent, stands and watches. The big tiger is also intrigued by this sheepish creature with the tiger's stripes. As the cub bleats and trembles, the big tiger realizes what might have happened, and talks to him, takes him to a nearby pool and shows him his own tiger face—tells him how the cub resembles him, the tiger, and not the sheep. He teaches him to growl and then to roar like a real tiger. The cub realizes who he really is as he hears his own full-throated roar, and goes with the older beast to the jungle to begin his real life.

Discovering that she is really the daughter of a king, he proposes to her and she accepts. But before she sleeps with him, she gets him to promise that if she should bear a son, he should be the heir apparent. He promises, makes love to her, and leaves. She does give birth to a son, and when he is 6 years old, Kaṇva sends mother and son to the king. The king rejects her, feigning ignorance of the secret marriage and contract, but Śakuntalā in a spirited speech accuses him of dishonesty. A voice from the sky confirms the truth of her claims, and the king is forced to accept her and her son—saying that he needed divine intervention, without which his acceptance would have been suspect.

Kālidāsa takes this story and turns it into a deeply psychological and subtle work on the nature of memory. He calls the play *Abhijñāna Śakuntalā*: the word *abhijñāna* means recollection, recognition. The word, with its variant *pratyabhijñāna*, is an old philosophic term, later reworked in Kashmiri Śaivism into an elaborate cosmology (Kaw *et al.*).* The history of this philosophy is not our present concern, nor are we saying as some have done that Kālidāsa himself was a Kashmiri and wrote this play to allegorize this philosophy (Kaw, 1967).* The relation of memory to cognition has been much discussed in various Indian systems. Some speak of four sources of true knowledge; *pratyakṣa* or direct perception, *anumāna* or inference, *smṛti* or memory, *āptavākya* or the verbal testimony of those who know (which the texts say may include foreigners). Others object that memory is not a true source of new knowledge: for it only re-presents what is already known. Anyhow, it is commonly agreed that even in direct perception of an object one needs memory to recognize it. The Sanskrit word has *prati*— as a prefix as the English one has *re*— in re-cognition. The philosophers further say that to recognize anything, one must remember having seen the object before, and remember a few features of it—these features trigger the memory of the whole object, or with the direct perception help us reconstitute it, literally re-member it. But it always needs a token, a mark, a sign. This is not just an abstract philosophic idea. In the Dravidian languages I work with, when we wish to say, 'Don't you remember me?' We say, '*gurutu sikkalillava?*' or, 'Didn't you get my mark *(gurutu)*?' When we wish to say, 'Don't forget it, hold it in your memory', we say, '*gurutu ittuko*', or 'Keep the mark *(gurutu, ataiyalam,*

*The two references to Kaw were left incomplete by AKR, as this essay was a work in progress.

etc.)'. Even the borrowed Sanskrit word for memory, *jñāpaka*, from the root *jñā* or know, has been syntactically enlisted into this paradigm: we use it as we use *gurutu* or mark and say, '*Jñāpaka ittuko*' meaning, 'Keep the mark, the memory'.

Now the Kālidāsa play plays in many ways with this mark, this triggering element without which no memory works (in this way of thinking). The central one, of course, is the ring that Duṣyanta has given his lover when he first met her, around which the whole action revolves. Let me now return to the story:

The play opens with Duṣyanta on a hunt. He enters the forest where Kaṇva's hermitage is situated, first as a hunter, later as a protector of the hermitage against marauding demons. He meets Śakuntalā, who lives among the trees and flowering plants as if she were one of them, tending the does and fawns as a foster mother, as she herself has been tended by Kaṇva and others as a foster child. Duṣyanta falls in love with her and she with him. They marry secretly according to one of the eight accepted modes of marriage, the *gandharva* mode, which is marriage by mutual consent without the presence of elders or priests. When he leaves, he asks Śakuntalā and her friends to keep his signet ring, and promises to send for her and make her his queen—even before they can count off the letters of his name engraved on it, day by day. Soon after he leaves, a sage known for his quick temper, Durvāsas, appears and Śakuntalā is too preoccupied with her love to attend to him; he gets furious and lays a curse on her: that the man she is thinking of should forget her. He later relents and adds that her lover will remember everything when he sees the ring he has given her. All this happens behind Śakuntalā's back and she does not hear of it.

When the king, stricken with the curse of amnesia as he is, does not send for her, Kaṇva sends Śakuntalā (who is now pregnant) to the king's court. In a dramatic scene at the court, Duṣyanta, troubled by undefined memories he cannot quite place, old recollections stirring obscurely within his amnesia, cannot remember her at all. She tries to show him the ring she had received from him—but it has meanwhile slipped from her finger and fallen into a holy river where she had bathed on her way. There is no 'mark' on her to activate his memory, as required by the curse. She, in a poignant effort, tries to find other reminders. She tries to remind him of a scene between them: when they were together in the hermitage, a little fawn would not take any water from his hands and came to Śakuntalā when she offered it. But Duṣyanta knows nothing of such an incident and thinks that it is a woman's cunning that has produced such a pretty scene to seduce him into accepting her. He repudiates her, and in her agony and incomprehension (for she knows nothing of the curse), she calls him unworthy of his race *(anārya)*, and calls upon her celestial mother who arrives to spirit her away to a heavenly abode.

In the next act, the sixth, a fisherman is caught with the lost ring—he has caught a fish and finds the ring in its belly. The bailiffs arrest him and bring the ring to the king, whose amnesia is at once cured, and he suffers a rush of memories and remorse at having repudiated the love of his life. He remembers, as he paints a picture of Śakuntalā from memory, little details like the bee that bothered her in the hermitage, the doe and the fawn that lay in the shade. But he cannot find his beloved anywhere, only marks of her, memories of her, all concentrated in the ring. In the seventh act, he is called by his friend Indra, the king of heaven, to assist him in battle. He again goes in his chariot (as he does in the first act), and after a victorious battle, finds himself in a hermitage. There he sees a boy playing rough with a lion cub—he experiences omens and physical sensations of love and kinship for the boy, who is really his son. Soon Śakuntalā appears, explanations follow, and the play ends in a family reunion.

The structure of the play is concentric: the first act is like the last, the second like the sixth, the third like the fifth, with the fourth at the centre (Edwin Gerow in Miller, 1984, p. 59; and Pollock, 1983, pp. 11–12).

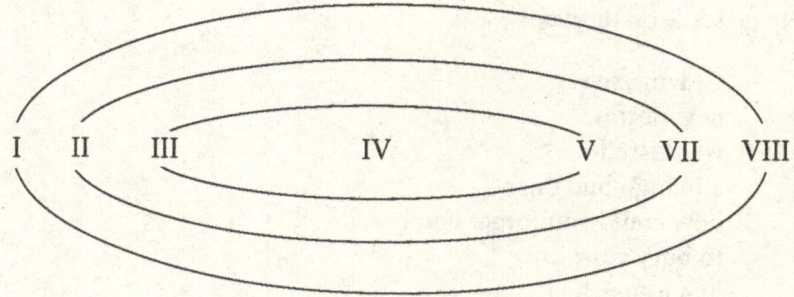

For instance, if the first act is union, the last is reunion; the second is full of the king's hopeful longing for Śakuntalā in her absence (she doesn't appear at all in that act), the sixth is full of his hopeless longings for her after he has recovered his memory and realized his mistake; the third act shows their physical union, his promise with the ring, and the curse, whereas the fifth act enacts their disunion and the loss of the ring and the fulfilment of the curse. In the fourth act, Kaṇva blesses her, and Śakuntalā takes leave of the forest trees that are her sisters and the animals that are her wards. The central four verses (Kaṇva's blessings on the new bride) are considered by the tradition as the centre of the play and the most moving in the context of envisaging a happy and loving family, the harmonious fulfilment of a good woman's dream. Even in little details, the first three acts are mirror-imaged by the last three: the first opens with the violence of Duṣyanta's hunt, the last with the violence of war; the first has Duṣyanta experiencing omens before he meets Śakuntalā, in the last he experiences them before he finds his son whom he has never seen before. These omens, the curse and the blessings (that he will have a great son), together with the metonymic emblems of the earlier scenes (the bee, the doe, the elephant, the flowering plants) that return later to remind him of his past—all these bind the narrative time, structure the future happenings, just as later the memories re-present the past.

Thus the first half sets up the experiences, and the second part relives them as memories through the marks and impressions and *vāsanās* (or smells) that those experiences have left behind. (Compare the structure of *Oedipus the King*, where, as the play's narrative time progresses, the narrated time regresses.) This reliving begins at the very beginning of the fifth act when Duṣyanta hears one of his women singing the following song, accusing him of being a fickle lover, a bee who has left one flower to go settle on the next:

> Craving sweet
> new nectar,
> you kissed
> a mango bud once—
> how could you forget her, bee,
> to bury your joy
> in a lotus?
>
> (Miller, 1984, V.1)

When he hears this song sung by one of his abandoned women, he understands the immediate context, but he is troubled by subconscious feelings beyond it. He says, without knowing what he is saying,

> Why did hearing the song's words
> fill me with such strong desire?
> I'm not parted
> from anyone I love ...
>
> Seeing rare beauty,
> hearing lovely sounds,
> even a happy man
> becomes strangely uneasy ...
> perhaps he remembers,
> without knowing why,
> loves of another life
> buried deep in his being ...
>
> (Miller, 1984, V. 2)

This verse also suggests that the power of a work of art consists in the way it triggers powerful unconscious memories, buried in the amnesia of daily life—almost like the ring of recollection. The *saṃskāras* or *vāsanās* that all experiences leave behind, that we carry with us everywhere, can be reactivated by these triggers. Through them, we remember, re-cognize what we have forgotten, re-integrate our negated past with the present. This is exactly what Duṣyanta does in the latter half of the play—as Barbara Stoler Miller (1984) says, 'The richly developed counterpoint of the final act is built from latent impressions of images and events that accumulate throughout the play' (p. 41).

When Duṣyanta has finally found Śakuntalā and reunited with her, he says to Mārīca, the sage of the hermitage,

> Like one who doubts the existence
> of an elephant who walks in front of him
> but feels convinced by seeing footprints,
> my mind has taken strange turns.
>
> (Miller, 1984, VII. 31)

In presence, there is often no perception, often because one is too close or preoccupied or cursed, as Duṣyanta was, with amnesia. But absence is filled with images of presence, especially if there are marks that excite memory. Memory always implies absence—even when we are reconstituting a present object, for we are comparing it with a previous perception, as the *pratyabhijñā* theory insists.

Just as memory is part of direct perception, to learn is to remember (whether it is the self or the Vedas), and to remember is to know the self, to forget is to be unaware of the self. Basavanna, the twelfth-century Vīraśaiva saint, says, in a poem that begins, *aridare śarana, maredare manava*:

> He who knows is a saint,
> but he who forgets is a mere man.
> Metal becomes a mirror
> when it is burnished,
> but just metal
> when it is tarnished

—capable of reflecting nothing. In Kannada usage, *mare* or 'forget' is not only the opposite of *nene*, 'remember', but also of *ari*, 'know'.

To remember is also to love or rather to love is to remember, as Duṣyanta demonstrates. So one name for the love god is *Smara* (memory). In one of the earliest occurrences of the word in the *Atharva Veda*, the word could be read both ways: a lovesick woman prays that god will send Smara, the god of love, maybe just memory, to her indifferent lover.

In Indian love poetry, absence is more intense than presence. The great love poems are all poems of separation (*vipralambha*), filled with memory and desire. Kālidāsa's long poem *Meghadūta* has for its subject a *yakṣa* (a supernatural being) who is cursed to be far away from his beloved. He pines for her, remembers the way to her place, and sends a cloud to journey in the same path and give her his message of love. The whole poem is devoted to his reconstructing not merely his memories of love for her but the actual geography of the route that one has to traverse before one can reach her—it is a map of memory, converting past time into present space, that one has to read before his messenger can reach her. In the *Rāmāyaṇa*, every relationship suffers from separation and distance and even loss: the father sees his son go into exile, the hero loses his wife to Rāvaṇa, a demonic kidnapper filling Rāma's eyes, wherever he turns, with images of the absent Sītā. His brothers and the entire citizenry of his kingdom miss his presence and wait for his return. Even the shorter love poems are largely about the lover's absence and are suffused with memories of his presence. Bilhana's *Caurapañcāśika* (Fantasies of a Love Thief) is a series of memories of lovemaking like the following:

> Even now,
> I remember her:
> deep eyes' glittering pupils
> dancing wildly in love's vigil,
> a wild goose
> in our lotus bed of passion—
> her face bowed low with shame
> at dawn.
> > (Miller, 1978, p. 106)

Hundreds of verses in Sanskrit and other Indian languages follow this formula of a lover's memories. In a remarkable Tamil poem in the *Ainkurunuru*, an unfaithful husband comes home in the morning to find the door shut in his face by his wife; he remembers his wedding night, sitting outside his house in the cold of dawn. The memory of his first night in the warmth of an inner room is framed poignantly by his present situation of stale infidelity, his wife (temporarily) shutting him out of her house:

> What He Said
> > *after a quarrel, remembering his wedding night*
>
> Serving in endless bounty
> white rice and meat
> cooked to a turn,
> > drenched in ghee,
> to honoured guests,
>
> and when the bird omens were right,
> at the perfect junction
> of the Wagon Stars with the moon
> > shining in a wide soft-lit sky,
>
> wedding site decorated, gods honoured,
> kettledrum and marriage drum
> sounding loud the wedding beat,
>
> the woman who'd given her a bridal bath
> –piercing eyes looking on, unwinking–
> suddenly gone,

                    her near kin
strung a white thread on her
with the split soft-back leaves
of the sirissa,
and with the *aruku* grass,

          its sacred root a figurine,
          its buds cool, fragrant,
          dark-petalled, blue
          as washed sapphire,

          brought forth by the thundering skies
          of first rains in valleys
          where adolescent calves
          feed on them,

they brought her to me
decked in new clothes,
rousing my desire
even in the wedding canopy,
          wedding noises noisy as pounding rain,

on that first night,

and when they wiped her sweat,
and gave her to me,
          she splendid with ornament,
          I said to her
          who was body now to my breath,
          chaste without harshness,
          wrapped all over in a robe
          new, uncrushed,

'It's hot. Sweat is breaking out
on that crescent, your brow.
Open your robe a little,
let the wind cool it,'

and even as I spoke,
my heart hasty with desire,
I pulled it off

and she stood exposed,
her form shining

like a sword unsheathed,
not knowing how to hide herself,

cried *Woy!*
in shame, then bowed, begged of me,
as she loosened her hair
undoing the thick colourful wreath
of broken lily petals

and, with the darkness of black full tresses,
hand-picked flowers on them
still luring the bees,

hid
her private
parts.

> Virrurru Muteyinanar
> *Akananuru* 136
> (Ramanujan, 1985, pp. 108–10)

Similarly, the elegies of the dead heroes are naturally poems of memory, marks and memorials as much as an edict or a stone edifice is. Here is a short example:

Waterfalls sounded
on one side,

and on another,

the clear liquor
spilling over
when poured into the bowls
of minstrels
would turn the stones in its stream
as it flowed

on the hill
of that sweet man
bitter only to enemy kings
with elephants
and many spears.

But no more

> Kapilar, Tamil, First century
> (Ramanujan, 1985, p. 148)

When these erotic and heroic traditions are enlisted in the service of religious poetry, with god as the divine lover and all of creation as his beloved, the poems again dwell on his absent presence, a void filled with memories of his presence: so *Virahabhakti* (Freidhelm Hardy's phrase for a devotion that flowers in landscapes of absence) looms larger than the *bhakti* of union, and religious poetry becomes a chant of his forms that are more than mere commemorations of him. For, the forms of creation are parts of him that *will* him into being as they are remembered. They act as metonymies, and in terms of *pratyabhijñāna*, as marks that help us conjure his presence in his absence. So *smaraṇa* or remembrance, a constant struggle with forgetting which perpetually fogs the mind, and with the distractions that lead it astray, becomes a technique for practicing the presence of god.

> you are the forest
>
> you are the great trees
> in the forest
>
> you are the bird and beast
> playing in and out
> of all the trees
>
> O lord white as jasmine
> filling and filled by all
>
> why don't you show me your face?
> > Mahādēviyakka
> > (Ramanujan, 1973, p. 122)

As Edward S. Casey (1992, p. 285) summarizes this way of thinking,

All experiences 'leave their mark'. Such experiences come marked: marked *for* memory and marked *by* memory. They are marked to be remarked; they are made to be remembered. Heidegger speaks of the human condition as being 'on the way to language'. Yet this is so only because to be on the way to memory is already to be on the way to language—on the way to marking, that as signing is the basis of language.

Of course, the most powerful remembrancer of an absent object is its name—especially if you consider that the name of an object is not merely an attribute, but a part of that object. A name is a metonym, a part that stands for the whole, especially a part that can be detached from the original and carried everywhere to conjure up the original at will. Hence to remember and recite a god's many names is to invoke him—and each name is a summary of one of his aspects or deeds or relationships, as Dāśarathi is the name of Rāma in his aspect as a son of Daśaratha, and Madhusūdana is the name of Kṛṣṇa as the slayer of a demon named Madhu; thus the sum of Viṣṇu's thousand names is Viṣṇu himself in his thousand facets; to recite them is to conjure his presence, to banish other presences that preoccupy the mind.

Nammālvār (ninth century, Tamil) thinks of god as ever-available, needing only a call, a mere name, even the memory of a place. To utter it is enough to conjure his presence:

> I just said,
> 'The grove and hill of my lord',
> and he came down
> and filled my heart.
> > 10.8.1.
> > (Ramanujan, 1981, p. 78)

References

Casey, Edward S. (1992). 'Remembering Resumed: Pursuing Buddhism and Phenomenology in Practice', in Janet Gyatso, ed., *In the Mirror of Memory, Reflections on Mindfulness and Remembrance in Indian and Tibetan Buddhism*. Albany: State University of New York Press.

Coomaraswamy, Ananda K. (1977). 'Recollection, Indian and Platonic', in Roger Lipsey, ed., *Coomaraswamy: Selected Papers*, vol. 2. Princeton: Princeton University Press.

Ingalls, D.H.H., *et al.*, trs. (1990). *The Dhvānyaloca of Anandavardhana with the Locana of Abhinavagupta*. Cambridge: Harvard University Press.

Kaw, R.K. (1967). *The Doctrine of Recognition (Pratyabhijna Philosophy)*. Hoshiarpur: Vishveshvaranand Institute.

Lopez, Donald. (1992). 'Buddha's Memory of Past Lives', in Janet Gyatso, ed., *In the Mirror of Memory, Reflections on Mindfulness and Remembrance in Indian and Tibetan Buddhism*. Albany: State University of New York Press.

Miller, Barbara S. (1978). *The Hermit and the Love-Thief.* New York: Columbia University Press.

——, ed. (1984), *Theater of Memory: The Plays of Kālidāsa.* New York: Columbia University Press.

Peterson, Indira. (1980). 'In Search of Past Lives: Karma and Rebirth in the Story Literature of India', (unpublished).

Pollock, S. (1983). 'What Happens in *Śakuntalā*', (unpublished).

Potter, Karl, ed. (1977). *Indian Metaphysics and Epistemology: The Tradition of Nyāya-Vaiśeṣika up to Gaṅgeśa. Encyclopedia of India Philosophies,* vol. 1. Princeton: Princeton University Press.

Ramanujan, A.K. (1973). *Speaking of Śiva.* London: Penguin books.

——. (1981). *Hymns for the Drowning: Poems for Viṣṇu by Nammāḷvār.* Princeton: Princeton University Press.

——. (1985). *Poems of Love and War.* New York: Columbia University Press.

FOR BARBARA MILLER *

———◆I◆◆———

I've always come to New York these twenty or more years to see Barbara at least once a year. I didn't imagine I would come to New York to visit her absence.

Like many others, I find it difficult to speak or write for difficult occasions. I fall into silence, remember trivia, like the etymology of trivia—that Barbara and I once talked about: Roman crossroads where three roads met, where the Romans put up posters for news. I escape into such crossroads, into dictionaries or dreamtalk full of puns, anything to forget the bed of thorns on which we've to lie now and then, anything at all interesting and irrelevant to shirk the task at hand, the hard work of mourning.

Suddenly the bed of thorns puts out a leaf, a flower, a memory of things that could only be said to this particular friend who lent me her ears several times a year through a black telephone in New York: like saying to her why I cannot finish a book of folktales that she had helped me begin,

> because cooks
> and grandmothers
> had fed me rice
> and ogres ...

*Two months before his own death, AKR delivered this eulogy.

or how

> Pierre Bonnard
> had only one model, his wife
> and he painted her all his life,
> even at seventy
> as if she was not a day older
> than thirty-six,
> stepping in and out
> of a bathtub
> on to diamond patterned
> violet tiles ...

when she laughed and said she turned 36 that week but didn't have a painter around (but later she did, a most loving and wonderful man who knew how to grow city trees, cement for earth, sulphur and smog for a sky, and he painted her into landscapes and the mirrors of water in autumn).

She liked stories, the upside-down Oedipus that a half-blind granny told me in Kittur, or the prince who went in search of truth and found her a hag, bent double in a forest cave, who gave him all her wisdom and when he asked for a message to be given to the world, said, 'Tell them I am young and beautiful'.

The *gulmohur* trees were all aflame in May, and the bed of thorns had one of those orange flowers; that look in her eyes when her little daughter was learning to dance in Mysore, my hometown, from a woman 70 years old who didn't even stand but sat down to mime love and longing with her eyes and body as if she were 17, shedding wrinkles and years with each movement of her eyebrow, seducing every man, woman, and child in that room into falling for this sexy playful unattainable beauty of 17 in a 70-year-old fat body with flowers in her gray hair, miming into my memory Sanskrit poems my friend was then making her own, the *Caurapañcāśika*, the *Love Song of the Dark Lord*, and Kālidāsa's poem on the way memory stirs in the depths of amnesia:

> Seeing rare beauty, hearing lovely sounds,
> even a happy man
> becomes strangely uneasy ...
> perhaps he remembers,

without knowing why,
loves of another life
buried deep in his being.

No death is easy, no death is acceptable, even to believers in immortal souls. We may quote and quote, 'Fear no more the winter's rages', yet all we can do is remember and count the number of good things she left behind: the distinguished life; a generation of students and colleagues whom she urged and often scolded in person and on the telephone into creative urgencies; hundreds of poems brought whole and alive from an ancient language which would be dead but for the art and magic of a translator like her, a lovely wholesome daughter reared with wholehearted care and thought; and friends who carry shining bits, fragrances, the taste of salads and pastas, walking through galleries of Moghul paintings, looking at squirrels scampering on a fig tree come alive on a museum wall in New York, making more alive the bushtails begging for crumbs outside the MET as we walk out; and I'll not speak of the dozens of committees, chairs, presidencies, lectures, books, honours, the Yogasūtras book she said to me she finished in the hospital. I'll speak only of a friendship begun thirty years ago, as if it was last week, in a train from Poona when she was 23, the manuscript of her first book in her hand, her daughter and every other kind of future only a gleam in her eye.

Suddenly I realize my trivia, the crossroads, the posters in Madras that cows love to peel and eat, the flowering trees of Mysore, the Moghul squirrels, all such trivia are lit, shaded, darkened by sadness on a spring day, by absent presences that we mourn, miss, yet feel blessed by their having been here so fully alive to such things.

8 May 1993

A NOTE ON A.K. RAMANUJAN'S
UNCOLLECTED POEMS

———◆◆◆◆◆———

The One Self Within the Many Selves

The thirty-two poems selected for this volume were chosen because they could be re-read; the excluded ones seemed to be surface verses, mostly writing exercises, yielding nothing on a second reading. The latter are in safekeeping at the University of Chicago's Regenstein Library.

In the opening poem, 'Invisible Bodies', each stanza has a person in it, four persons in all, a man and a woman, a boy and a girl: *he, she, the boy,* and in the last stanza, *the girl* twirling her parasol. *He* sees 'three newborn puppies/in a gutter with a mother curled around them'. If this is a metonymy for *his* life, then one might say that *he* has been loved. The woman in the second stanza 'found a newborn naked baby,/male, battered, dead in the manhole/with no mother around'. The word 'naked' colours the line. Perhaps it is a metonymy for her life; she might be the abandoned newborn baby, a common feeling in a great many women; or is the male infant, the male part of her psyche, abandoned, battered, snuffed out over a lifetime? There is nothing in the poem to suggest that she is projecting the image as her view of the man in the first stanza, or of the boy in the third stanza. These people are not relating to each other, they exist eerily connected by the consciousness of another at a particular place and time.

Is the boy in the third stanza a younger version of the *he*? Or is the boy an actual person in the real world, where the street stands for his life, as say Raskolnikov's room stands for his world? Is the boy's life littered with junkies and crotch-sniffing dogs? Perhaps the boy too is looking at the mirror of the self. The two males in the poem, the man and the boy, exist in the poem, and there is no reason to think that the male infant is the woman's projected image about the man. Everything in the poem is being seen by the speaker. Furthermore, the repetition of the opening phrase, 'Turning the corner', three times as the opening phrase of each stanza, suggests to this reader that these might be different masks for the same person, who then sees the opposite of the three, the fourth self, enticingly present though absent.

In the fourth stanza the speaker omits 'Turning the corner' and says, at all times, even on yellow-leaved fall days, the girl under the twirling parasol is oblivious to all this. Who is she? Perhaps she is Elvira who appears on a tightrope with a twirling parasol (AKR's image from a movie he saw and used in a poem earlier), or could she belong with the other three—man, woman, and boy? As a double, could she be the younger self whom the speaker envies because of her lack of oppressive consciousness? Is she one of the many selves within the one self?

All the personae, including the speaker, are connected by place, but each is locked into individual seeing. Nothing escapes the speaker of the poem; he sees them all. Everything presses upon his consciousness. For the poem to work, the connections are to be made by the reader, who must see that the speaker is the opposite of *the girl*.

Is the speaker presenting the self and the non-self? Could the personal in the poem be parts of the speaker? Are they a metaphor for the splits within him?

Is the speaker concurrently the loved newborn puppy, and the abandoned motherless battered male? Is he the street kid among the junkies? Could he also be the 'girl under the twirling parasol' unaware of all the images that press upon his nerves? Could the girl be the *non-you* of the poem? Or is she the anti-self within the *you*? A case could be made for either or both of these ideas.

In the first half of the poem, the poet presents the world outside the self: the newborn puppies with 'a mother curled/around them' and the newborn naked baby, 'battered dead in the manhole/with no mother around'. In the second half of the poem, do the boy and the girl present aspects of the self? These aspects, the self-in-the-world, the self-as-world, and the self-removed-from-the-world, are seen in the boy and the girl. The boy is not removed from the rubble of life; he walks on junkie strewn streets, but the unseeing girl sees none of the ugliness. She, an enticing girl twirling her parasol, is the opposite of the seer in the poem; she is the relief; she stands at the opposite pole. Could she be the untouched and untouchable self?

Poets give to 'airy nothings' a 'habitation and a form'. Can poetry be created by the girl removed from the life around her? If so, what would the image-making self feed on? Do the splits in the speaker give him entry into fourfold views? Is this what was meant by the phrase, 'multiplying variety in a wilderness of mirrors'?

And finally, in a Hindu flourish, may we wonder if the dogs, the naked abandoned battered male infant, the grown boy, the junkie he stepped over, the girl, and even the 'gamboge maples' are invisible bodies to the Great Seer? And if they are invisible, do they exist, and for whom? Presumably, the title is given by the poet, not the speaker. This creates a paradoxical distance between the speaker and the poet. Is the poet the Great Seer?

The answers to these somewhat unanswerable questions may be further compounded by the enormity of the vision in 'Oranges'. The whole of life, of nature, cycles of birth and death, all can be seen in the oranges on top of the refrigerator. AKR, who loved fruit more than most, often left it on top of his refrigerator to suffer painful neglect and become mouldy. Note that 'Oranges' donates to the speaker a real object from the poet's very real life. But in the poem, the oranges are replicated in parallel entries about cycles of regeneration. AKR was aware of two simultaneous truths: a) the whole cosmos could be seen in a drop of water, and b) the drop of water was also the mirror in which he saw himself. The mould on the oranges is the individual destiny as well as the collective. In widening circles the images in Ramanujan's poetry show him to be the poet of consciousness, the poet of the consciousness of self. His poems reiterate: consciousness is all we have.

Life into Poems

Rejected poems, like rejected lovers, can be more illuminating than others. The poem 'Turning Around' was included at the last minute in *The Black Hen* in *Collected Poems,* plucked out of the rejects for a reason. It casts a certain light on the process of the poet's imaginings. The flock of sheep are real sheep seen on a Himalayan slope in Pahalgaum, Kashmir, in 1972. They are being sheared before they are taken to the slaughterhouse. The sheep collect under the trees, their heads pressing together. So great is this impression that they seem to have conjoined heads. Their prescient sense of doom and their recognition of imminent extinction form a sort of impenetrable heavy air around them like a mountain mist. The sheep could easily have been people. That haunting moment was palpable.

Now, consider what the poet makes of this 19 years later. He notes: the shepherd is doing what he has to do, as his father before him has done, grandfather to father to son, emulations that are time-honoured in the subcontinent. Looking on, the speaker has a Hamletian thought: what is the viewer to the viewed? He asks,

> but what am I to this herd
> of Indian sheep, to be fed
> and sheared or
>
> slaughtered, or to this man
> who shares a throaty cry
> with his father
>
> and his father's father,
> his cousins and enemies
> for miles around?

As in 'Invisible Bodies', one notices that the displaced man, the visitor, a seer of the other's life, a person apart, finds himself among disparate images, and sees connections. As poet, he can 'connect' by making metaphoric or metonymic leaps. This is a self-sustaining act. It needs no fuel, but it fuels the creativity of the poet. Eventually a poem is born through a concerted act of consciousness—the consciousness of the self, as reflected in a fractured world, comes together through the power of words.

AKR's Spoken Voice

The interviews in the book are lively, and AKR's voice resonates in them. The magic is that it is the same voice even though the interviews were conducted 20 years apart. But nowhere does the poet's very human presence come across as fully as in his eulogy of his close friend and colleague, Barbara S. Miller. And noticeably, in talking of death, AKR is talking of life.

Molly A. Daniels-Ramanujan

INDEX OF TITLES

———◆◆◆———

INDEX OF FIRST LINES